MOVIN' UP

POP GORDY TELLS HIS STORY

MOVIN' UP

BY BERRY GORDY, SR.

HARPER & ROW, PUBLISHERS

New York

Cambridge
Hagerstown
Philadelphia
San Francisco

London
Mexico
Sao Paolo
Sydney

1817

Movin' Up: Pop Gordy Tells His Story

FIRST EDITION

Library of Congress Cataloging in Publication Data
Gordy, Berry, 1888–1978.
    Movin' up, Pop Gordy tells his story.

    SUMMARY: The autobiography of Berry Gordy, Sr., son
of a slave and father of the founder of Motown Records.
    1. Gordy, Berry, 1888–1978—Juvenile literature.
2. Afro-Americans—Michigan—Detroit—Biography—
Juvenile literature.   3. Afro-Americans—Georgia—
Biography—Juvenile literature.   4. Detroit—Biography
—Juvenile literature.   5. Georgia—Biography—
Juvenile literature.   6. Country life—Georgia—
Juvenile literature.   [1. Gordy, Berry, 1888–1978.
2. Afro-Americans—Biography]   I. Title.
F574.D49N4433   1979   301.45'19'6073024 [B] [92]   78-22493
ISBN 0-06-022053-8
ISBN 0-06-022054-6 lib. bdg.

"Life is somethin'. Life is really somethin'. You just got to know how to live it. There's lots to learn."

Berry Gordy, Sr.

Dedicated to the memory of my dear and beloved wife, Bertha Ida, who was my best helpmate all through life; and also to my children, who all turned out good.

INTRODUCTION

"POP" Gordy was such a father figure to so very many of us who knew and loved him—not only his family, but literally thousands of others from different walks of life. Whenever any of us would feel the need to talk with this man, it was because we felt in him a kind of combination of strength, goodness, wisdom, and understanding such as is seldom possessed by any one human being. We knew that we had only to pick up a telephone and visit with Pop conversationally, if we did not wish to go and sit with him personally. Today a sense of his *presence* certainly is very much with every one of us who had the honor and the privilege to know him.

If *Movin' Up* is to be your first meeting with Pop, then it is important that you understand it represents highlights of his long life as he recalled them in a number of tape-recorded sessions; and also that this Pop Gordy was a man who never attempted to be "fancy" in anything he ever said, or that he ever did, for that matter. For throughout his life, Pop was as simple, direct, and straightforward as he was honest, candid, and sincere.

If you are to get the most out of Pop's memories, which he shares with us here, you should realize that much of what Pop is telling us about are experiences of his boyhood, youth, and young manhood; he is, in fact, giving us a look at how peoples' lives went scores of years ago in the part of Georgia where he was reared. You might want to compare Pop's experiences with your own and consider whether and how much manners of expression and relationships between the races have changed since the time of Pop's childhood."

In Pop's boyhood world, his father was one of the many men who farmed with their families' help within the general area of small Sandersville, Georgia. But where most farmers ended each year once more in debt to the bank and various credit merchants, in the Gordys' case it was different. Pop and his brothers and sisters grew up seeing the practically religious regard of their parents for keeping meticulous records of any business they were involved in, no matter how seemingly trivial or small. As one result, the Gordys were gradually able to save enough to buy more land, and a better home to live in. So the principles of hard work and careful business practices were early and indelibly impressed upon the Gordy children.

Physically small for his age, Pop (or little Berry)

also learned how to use his quick fists to gain respect. To be sure, he loved his pranks and mischief, which brought him frequent switchings and whippings from one or the other of his parents. You must chuckle when Pop recollects his bumbling, futile efforts to lie to his daddy about how a dog had attacked a cat that had killed an "invisible" rabbit. Or you can't help be tickled as he steals his fill of his mother's preserves, which she had thought he thoroughly disliked; and at his efforts to prevent his first girl friend's discovery that he and his brother and sister had to walk for miles to get home from high school. You will pull for Pop's battling school-yard bullies, until he finally beat their biggest and toughest, thus earning their respect and even their friendship.

Pop's father somehow sensed in him the special potential of a businessman, and let Berry accompany him into town to do the necessary "figgerin' " when business was conducted with various merchants. Berry developed the habit that when not working, he spent much of his free time alone, simply thinking about things he had read, seen, or heard—especially things he had overheard from local elderly people, particularly his beloved grandma. Later he would tell his own children that he found that listening quietly to elderly people's conversations had taught him as much as anything he had ever learned in school.

No part of this book is more emotionally moving than Pop's account of the tragic, abrupt death of his father, which left their whole family feeling ravaged. But it would seem as if his father had been training

Berry to become the "administrator" who would attend to family affairs. It was soon locally circulated that the young Berry was nobody's fool.

Meeting a pretty local schoolteacher named Bertha Fuller, young Berry Gordy convinced her that she should marry him. He expanded his business activities. He sold beef from a cart. He raised and sold pigs. Then when he sold for his family a large number of timber stumps from their joint property, he feared to cash the resulting $2600 check anywhere locally, lest it cause problems, and upon advice he took a long train ride to cash the large check in Detroit.

After Pop was married, he moved his family to Detroit. You will read how Pop taught himself to plaster and to do carpentry, until he became a contractor. He bought a grocery store, which became a small institution within the east side Detroit black community.

Pop and his good wife, Bertha, continued their job of raising a family of eight children with such quality that they would live to see their family acclaimed as one of the most outstanding black families within the nation. Among their children, the next to youngest son, Berry Gordy, Jr., who is the chairman of the board of Motown Industries, one of the major forces within the world of American popular music, said recently, "I express the opinions of my brothers and sisters on very few subjects—except Pop.

"What meant most to all of us, I think, was how Pop instilled into us what *work* meant. He was such a strong human being, a strong person, he was a living symbol and example for us. He taught us always to support what was right, what was fair. His philosophy was one of his favorite sayings: 'If you're right, fight!' "

Added Berry Gordy, Jr., "When people have said or written things to imply that *I* made Pop, they couldn't be more wrong. The truth is that whatever I am, Pop made *me*."

Pop had his executive-suite office on Motown's eighteenth floor, and it soon became known that if anyone at all had some problems to discuss, there was a willing ear in Pop Gordy. The people who turned to him ranged from unknown young recording artists to some of the topmost stars in the business.

In a rare testimonial, four of the greatest stars in the nation—Diana Ross, Stevie Wonder, Marvin Gaye, and Smokey Robinson—joined in making a recording titled "Pops, We Love You!" which became a rapid-selling single, although it was done as a birthday tribute for Pop in which the four stars expressed the sentiments of the many hundreds whose lives Pop had touched.

Then one midnight, Pop's daughter Anna telephoned her brother Berry, Jr., saying that she was visiting Pop, who had indigestion. Berry went over, and the three of them talked into the wee hours, until Pop Gordy fell asleep. The next morning he arose ready for breakfast, but in an hour he was dead.

As his son Berry, Jr., says, "Pop was a man whom not one of us ever had seen depressed, not for one moment of his life. We had never known him without his humor, and his wit, so the sadness usually associated with funerals just didn't seem right. And so we didn't have any funeral in the usual sense. We had a celebration. We just gathered with Pop there, and we talked about Pop."

The Gordy family was only acting out what had been one of the favorite sayings of Pop, that he had told to so many of his friends and admirers. "You can give without loving," Pop would say, "but you cannot love without giving."

ALEX HALEY
1979

MOVIN' UP

CHAPTER ONE

NOW, my great-grandfather, on my mother's side, was an Indian, and his wife was a colored lady. My father's mother was named Esther Johnson, who probably was a slave. Esther Johnson and my grandfather, Jim Gordy, didn't get married. He was a white man, a plantation and slave owner.

I was crazy about my grandmother. She lived in a little house out from our house. I used to see my father carrying her something to eat down there. He'd go to the smokehouse and get a bucket of flour and a ham. He'd just take her some food, take care of her. Sometimes I'd be 'round there, and I'd just go in the smokehouse and get something and take it to her myself. She cooked sorghum molasses and biscuits. Didn't have no little cute biscuits like they have now. She made big biscuits, as big as two or three of what they have now. But they were good, though. I really don't know how old she lived to be. She might have been in her seventies. She passed away a long time ago, when I was very small. I didn't know my grandfather, Jim Gordy. He was living, I reckon, I think at the time I was a small boy. But I never did meet him.

I guess we all are colored. I don't know exactly. Now, my wife is colored, my children, my grandchildren, and my great-grandchildren are colored. My brothers and sisters are all colored. We don't know anything but being colored people.

My mother's name was Lucy Hellum, and she married my father, Berry Gordy. He was a very nice, loving person, a businessman. He could read, write good. He figgered, too. He had a pretty good education, but I don't know how that come about. He had good "mother-wit," you know, good judgment.

And my father's temper, well, he would fight if you pressed 'im. But only if you pressed 'im. You would have to make him fight, and he would. On my mother's side of the family, though, if you would ask for a fight, you could get a good one in a hurry. They would fight anybody; they didn't pick and choose. If anybody mistreated anybody on my mother's side, the color of the skin didn't mean anything, they would get a fight.

My mother was six or seven years old when freedom was declared. My father was, maybe, eight or ten years old. They had altogether twenty-three children. Course, all of them didn't get grown. Some died 'fore I was born, died babies, and some of them died after I was born. The oldest one was my brother, Sam Gordy. My oldest sister Lula, I nicknamed her "Sister." Then there was Esther, then Mamie, then me, then Lucy, who we called "Nig," then John, Joe, and my brother Charlie, who was the baby.

We lived in the country in Oconee, Georgia. The house we lived in was a log house. If you wanted to see the sunrise, you could lay in bed and look through the cracks and see the sun when it rose. Then if you wanted to hear and see the chickens, you could sit and look through the cracks in the floor and see them walking back and forth beneath the house. Our house was very open with large cracks in the roof and floors. We never was suffering for fresh air 'cause there we had aplenty all the time coming through the cracks. It was very healthy.

Papa was a good businessman, ran his own business. He didn't depend upon the white people to get things or do things for 'im. He'd do just the same as the white folks. He'd make his arrangements and do his farming and everything. He was just his own boss. My father was enslaved until 'bout ten years old. He didn't inherit anything that I knowed of. When we were born, we lived on a plantation. Papa was renting the place from Mr. Sweeny, a white man. But Papa worked himself up by his own work. After he raised seven or eight children, after we got a little size, he bought his own plantation and run his business just like white folks. He bought him 168 acres.

Papa was well liked and a well-known businessman. Most of the people in his town, especially the colored and a lot of the poor white people, would have to sell their crops every year to pay their debts. All year they would be trading with the country store, buying food and things for the year, and they would pay for it all in the fall. The people would have a lot of stuff charged to 'em on the books in the store. Some of 'em didn't know what they had gotten. They didn't keep account. The white man would figure their bill up. The colored folks depended on him to keep the books, and they believed whatever he said. But the white man would keep the colored people in debt. Plenty of the people were like that. The first of every year, they'd have to start another crop. They'd start out already owing the white man some money. I never did hear tell of any of these people paying their debts off.

Well, my father had records. He always kept receipts. He didn't throw away anything. That's the part my mother played. He taught her to save all receipts; never throw away a receipt. She took care of this part. She couldn't read or write, but she knowed business. She had "mother-wit" too.

When I was 'bout six years old, my father started me to work. In fact all of us children had to work when we were in elementary school. We would go to school every day, and we would have to work evenings after school. In the summer months, when the days were long, we often would work an hour before school and then again in the afternoon. Mama and Papa kept us working all the time, but they would mostly let us rest on Saturday evenings. We followed that routine 'til we finished elementary school.

One Saturday evening we wanted to get off to go hunting. Papa wanted us to work, but we begged 'im to let us go hunting. He said, "Aw, ya'all ain't gon' kill nothing." But we told him, "Yeah, Papa, we sure gon' kill something. We'll kill something." So, Papa decided to let us go hunting.

We hunted all that evening, and we didn't kill a thing. So, 'long 'bout sundown, we saw that we wasn't gonna kill nothing. We didn't know what in the world to do. Then we saw a cat out 'cross the field, and we put the dog on the cat. The cat ran and tried to make it to a tree, but the dog caught her 'fore she got there. They fought awhile and the cat scratched and cut the dog, but the dog whipped the cat 'til it was near 'bout dead. The cat was near 'bout dead! So I made the dog get off the cat. My younger brothers wanted me to let the dog kill the cat. But I said, "Naw, I don't want to let 'im kill her." I told 'em, "I'll make up a story to tell Papa. I'll tell him why we didn't bring a rabbit or something back." Then I told my brothers the story I was gonna tell Papa.

I was gonna tell Papa we killed a rabbit and hung him up in a tree. Then, while we were hunting for another rabbit, the cat come and ate the rabbit up. So then the dog jumped on the cat 'bout eating the rabbit up. So that's why we didn't bring a rabbit back. Well, all my brothers agreed to help me tell the story. They were gonna be my witnesses. We had everything cut and dry. In the fight, the cat had split the dog's ear all up. The dog's ear was all bloody and bleeding. One of the dog's legs was really white, but now it was red from the blood dripping on it from his cut ear. So . . . the dog ran on back to the house.

Papa was out in the buggy shelter when we got back, and just happened to have a plowline in his hand. He did the whupping with a plowline, but we wasn't thinking of getting no whupping. When we got there, Papa was just looking at the dog and he saw that his ear was just dripping blood, just dripping, dripping, and his leg was just all bloody.

Papa said, "What's the matter with that dog?" I said, "Pa, aw aw a aw killed the rab—I mean the dog —a wa eat up the cat . . . naw, ra a cat eat up er er a ra, the rabbit, naw, naw. . . ." Papa said, "Shut up! Shut up!" 'Fore I could get my story out, Papa was whupping me with the plowline. POW! POW!

Now my brother John was a big fellow. He was outside of the buggy shelter, outta my father's sight. And he was leaning up against the wall just laughing. He was laughing so hard he couldn't stand up. He had his eyes closed, laughing himself to death! Papa got through whupping me, and he was so mad, he just walked out of the buggy shelter. He looked and saw John leaning up against the wall with his eyes closed, just laughing. Papa said, "Boy, what's the matter with you?!" He started whupping Johnny, too. John yelled out, he started hollering and crying. If he hadn't been

8

laughing, he wouldn't have got no whupping, 'cause I was at fault 'cause I was the oldest. But he was laughing, so Papa whupped him. He didn't whup Brother Joe. Boy, after everything was over and Papa was gone, it was funny. Papa whupped us good! It hurt then. We were laughing 'bout the whupping and laughing at one another. I was laughing at John 'cause he thought he was out of sight and Papa wouldn't see him. They was laughing at me 'cause my story didn't go over. And so that's the way it went.

I was born July the tenth, eighteen and eighty-eight. I'm a Cancer. Cancer people suppose to be good family people, good, hearty, and friendly. Since my father's name was Berry Gordy, he named me Berry Gordy. There's no middle name; none of the Berry Gordys have no middle name. I was in the middle somewhere; I was the fifth child of the ones was living.

When I was a boy, I thought for myself. A lotta times I would be around playing, and I would listen at the old people talk. I learned a lot from old people, but they didn't know I was listening at 'em. Lotta times, the rest of the children would be playing out in the yard, and I would be in the house playing or playing outside close 'round the house. My mother used to say I could play very good by myself. Said she didn't see how come sometimes the rest of the children were all one place playing, and I was playing 'round the house. I wouldn't be listening, trying to get nothing outta what the old people were saying, but I would just hear 'em. You hear 'em saying and talking 'bout things. They think the kids are not paying any attention to 'em. But kids hear what you say and hear good and they don't forget it.

My father used to always take me 'round with him when I was a boy, if I wasn't in school. He mostly went to town on Saturday. After we would get into town, he would have me doing the figgering for him. He would go down there and sell stuff from the farm and have me figger it out for 'im. I was a very good figgerer, very good. When we had cotton to sell, he would just tell me so many bales at so many pounds and have me figger out how much it amounts per pound. I would figger it out and would tell him what it was.

Sometimes he test me out. He would say, "Are you right?" I'd tell him I think so. Then I would go to figgering it again, to check it. He would look at my figgers and say, "You sure this right?" I'd tell him to wait just a minute, I'd figger it again. He'd say, "Oh, yeah, you're right. You were right the first time. After you have taken time to make sure you are right, and somebody ask you, say, 'Yes, I'm right.' You always let the figgers talk when you know what you are doing. If you know you are right, you don't have to go back. Don't care what anybody says. Go right ahead and tell 'em." I said, "Yes, suh." When you know you are right, stick to it. Don't care what nobody says. Stick to it.

Now my daddy was mostly a farmer. He used to raise and sell cotton. He raised cotton, corn, peas, potatoes, and he sold fruit. He had a peach orchard and he shipped peaches. He also raised sugarcane and sorghum cane for syrup, and peanuts, cabbage, collards,

okra—all the greens. He had a couple orchards of muscadines, but he didn't ship none of 'em, but we'd have
'em. He had cattle and hogs for us. And chickens. He'd
take a load of stuff to town to sell, like peddlin', and
he'd take chickens sometimes and eggs. He'd sell just
about anything people want to buy.

When I was 'bout seven or eight, I used to like eggs,
and Mama wouldn't hardly give us any eggs. She didn't
think we should eat eggs. Anyhow, I was begging her for
an egg one day. I had seen different folks roast eggs.
They would put 'em in the fire or wrap 'em up in a wet
rag and put the wrapped egg in the ashes and cover it
up. After a little while, they would take the egg out and
peel it, salt it, and eat it. So I asked Mama for an egg
one day, she was outside washing clothes in one of these
big, old, black metal pots that sat over a hot fire. I
wanted to roast an egg so bad. I continued to beg Mama
for an egg. She wouldn't give me any.

Finally, she walked up the hill to her sister-in-law's,
Aunt Cora, who we used to call "Tody." I waited 'til
Mama was out of sight, then I got me a rag and wet it,
went to the henhouse, and got me an egg. I wrapped the
egg up in the rag and put it in the ashes. I was playing
around waiting for the egg to cook. I happened to look
up and see my mother coming back down the hill head-
ing toward the house. I ran and got the egg outta the
fire and threw the rag away and ran and put the egg
back in the henhouse in the hen's nest. Soon as Mama
got back, I asked her for an egg again. She said, "All
right, go and get you one." So I went and got the same

11

egg I had and was wrapping it up in the rag. She saw me wrapping it, and she said, "Berry, you ain't wrapping that egg right." I tried to tell her that it was all right, that I could do it. "Oh, no you ain't. Gimme, gimme the egg," she said.

I was pleading with her, saying that it was all right, I could do it. She just came and took the egg outta my hand and said, "This egg is hot!" Then, she felt it again, cracked it, and said, "This egg is done! What this egg doing being done?" I told her that I didn't know. I reckon the hen laid it done. She didn't say no more, and she didn't whup me 'bout it; she just fixed the egg up and let me eat it. After then, whenever I ask for something, she would usually always give it to me. I guess that incident must of had some meaning to her.

Every time Mama left home, I would always think 'bout something to do. One day I thought 'bout going into the pantry, eating some preserves. So I went in there, pulled the chair up to the safe where my mother kept the preserves, and climbed up. I took the lid off a jar, took me a spoon, and I ate up 'bout half a jar of preserves. Then I wiped my mouth, fastened the lid, got down, and went out and played.

Mama came back, and she looked and saw where somebody had been in her preserves. She asked about it and none of the children knowed anything 'bout it. She said, "Well, some of you know, because it was in here when I left. I'm going to whup all of you 'cause I know some of you did it, and I know I'll get the right one." She whupped ev-

eryone but me, 'cause she thought I didn't like preserves.

We would get served preserves 'bout once a week,
on Sunday morning. We used to have preserves and nice
hot biscuits and butter. Mama would come 'round every
Sunday morning and put the preserves in everybody's
platter. When she'd stop to put some in my plate, I'd
say that I didn't want any. She'd say, "Oh, I forgot.
Berry don't like preserves." So she'd go on. She'd give
'em all preserves but me. So whenever Mama would
leave again, I'd go in the safe and eat some more preserves. I'd be full of preserves. I didn't want any when
she'd serve the rest of the family. That way she thought
I didn't like preserves when I wouldn't take any. Never
did take any at the table. It was a long time 'fore Mama
found me out 'bout that!

Another day Mama went off and left me in the
house alone. The rest of my brothers and sisters was
outside playing. I had played with the clock, turned the
alarm on, and let it ring as much as I wanted. I got tired
of that and I thought what else I could do. There was
a twenty-four-pound bag of sugar under the bed. I went
and dragged the bag 'side the bed. Then I laid down on
the bed and went to gnawing a hole in the sugar sack.
I chewed and chewed 'til I got a hole big enough where
I could stick my tongue into the sugar. I started licking
and eating the sugar. I just stayed there with my mouth
at the sugar-bag hole. Every time I eat one mouthful up,
I'd stick my tongue in there and get another tongue full.
The sack had got wet all around that hole.

I was there maybe 'bout half an hour eating sugar, and after a while, all of a sudden I heard somebody at the door. I looked up and seen my mother come in the door. I turned my head over right quick with my face up toward the ceiling like I was 'sleep. I didn't think she would talk to me if I was 'sleep. But she had saw me moving. She came in and pulled her hat and things off and said, "What's the matter with you, Berry?" I just acted like I was 'sleep, and I didn't say nothing. She said, "What's the matter with you?" And then I kinda turned over just like I was waking up, and she said, "What you doing in that sugar!" She grabbed me! You see, when I turned over, she saw my mouth where the sugar done stuck all to my jaws, and my face was full of sugar. She saw the sugar wasted all in the bed, and the wet sack. She pulled me outta bed and gave me a good whupping. Then she got the bag of sugar and put it away.

Now, my mother whupped us good when she whupped us. She'd go outdoors and get some sugarberry switches. She would stick 'em in warm ashes for a second or two to make 'em limber so they wouldn't break so easy. Then she would make us pull off our clothes and whup us good.

Sometimes, if we did something wrong and my mother didn't want to whup us, she would make us "highbob." She'd say, "Well, you highbob now. You got to highbob." Highbobbing is jumping up and down in one place, and at the same time saying, "Now, Mr. Princess, is the time to catch your nigger." I don't know whether we said nigger or nickel, but I think it was nigger. We sure did hate to highbob. Sometimes other children would all be standing 'round. You sure hated to jump up in front of them. They'd all be waiting to get a big laugh. Mama say, "Jump up and say it now, say it now!" You'd hate that 'cause you know the kids gonna laugh. Mama would act like she was gonna whup you. You would be 'bout to cry, but you'd start jumping and saying in a whining voice, "Now, Mr. Princess, is the time to catch your nigger." She might make us say it over and over again. So the kids all laugh and Mama didn't whup us.

We really didn't have any bad or lazy children in the family, though. When our parents tell us to do something, they meant it, and we knowed it. We'd go ahead and do it. If we were lazy, why, we didn't show it much. They'd give us a prize for whoever do this or that first. Oh, it was nothing much: sardines and a box of crackers, something like that. You would work for that prize. They knew how to handle us pretty well. We'd work hard, you know. I think all of us worked 'cause we had to.

Back then my father also had a cane mill and an evaporator. He learned me how to make syrup. In winter when it was syrup-making time, he let me travel with the mill and make all of the syrup for him. We would go three or four miles from our home and set up there. Everybody in that neighborhood would haul their cane to us, and I would make up all the syrup in each location. I'd make several hundred gallons, then we would move to another neighborhood and do the same thing. You'd put the cane into the cane mill, grind the juice out of it, and then put the juice into the evaporator. You'd then put fire under the furnace and cook the juice and make syrup. He used to do this for people all 'round the neighborhood there where we lived. People would bring their cane to my father, and we would make up all of their syrup. We'd get toll for it—every eight gallons we got a gallon.

We did sort of the opposite when we wanted cornmeal. We would shuck the corn by taking all the leaves and silk off it. Then we would put the ear of corn into the corn sheller, which would separate the grain of corn from the cob. Then we would take the corn grains to the gristmill and have the corn grains ground up into cornmeal. We would bring the meal home and sift it to get fine cornmeal. In our house, we used to have a big wood fireplace with a big chimney built out of stick and dirt and stick and mud. We would have those good old oak fires, and we would sometimes cook ashcakes made out of cornmeal.

We take some cornmeal, put it in a bowl or crock. We then season it with salt and a pinch of soda, mix it up with buttermilk and maybe a little water 'til we would get a soft batter. Then, we go over to the chimney and rake back the ashes and pour in some batter. You would rake the hot ashes back over the batter, and let it stay there long enough for the heat from the ashes to cook the cornmeal batter. Now the seasoning from that oak would get into that bread called ashcake. After the bread was done, you would take it out of the ashes, let it cool off a little bit 'til it was sorta hard on the outside, sorta like crust. Then you take some water and wash all the ashes off the ashcake and eat it. It taste just like, oh, just like pound cake.

We would also roast potatoes like that. We used to have a lot of fun playing a game called potato lice. You could take the potato outta the fire and ask anybody, "Have you ever seen any potato lice?" If they said no, you would take the potato and say, "Look right here." When they would bend over to look, you'd blow ashes in their faces, just blow it in their faces. Playing potato lice was a lot of fun.

When we was kinda grown, my daddy left the Sweeny place and bought his own batch of land which was 168 acres. Then he bought this plot of land of 100 acres which had on it this big white house, a big store, and everything that you can name that you use on a farm, everything that you need to stock a country store. Then my father bought all kinds of candy goods to put in the store.

The store had so much candy and different kinds; sixty-gallon kegs full of candy, with little small boxes full of candy—peppermint, lemon, and all kinds. So we was happy and started begging my father for candy. As soon as he got the keys every morning to open the store, we said, "Papa, give us some candy, please, sir." He said, "All right, help yourself there." He let us eat all the candy we wanted. We just know we was gonna have a big time eating candy. For three or four days we was just regular eating candy, eating candy.

We ate so much candy, after a while we got so we didn't love candy. We had ate ourselves out. We just all got gorged out. We got so we never did bother the candy. At first, we was just like hogs sitting 'round there waiting for Papa to open up the store. We ate so much candy it made us sick, I reckon. After that, he didn't have to worry 'bout us eating up the candy. From then on, he had plenty of candy to sell all the time.

CHAPTER TWO

When we all finished with grade school, we would have to work a few years 'fore Papa would send us back to high school. Sam and Lula and Esther, they went up to the high school in Sandersville, and the rest of us, we was working. And then after they finished school, later on, he sent three more to school. And that was me, my brother Johnny, and my sister Mamie. So I was 'bout twenty-two or so when I started to high school.

School was easy for me, yeah, it was easy. When I went to high school, I learned so much faster than when I was in grade school, 'cause I was interested and I know what education means to you. I don't know if my father paid for us to go. Maybe so. I don't remember. He took care of us, sent us to school. At that time I learned, I needed it. I didn't have any problems in school 'bout studying. Studied hard, we learned fast. I learned more in that time than I ever knew. I learned quite a bit.

When I went to high school, they touched on almost everything: agriculture, science, geography, history, reading, grammar, and arithmetic. I was a good science scholar and good in arithmetic, figuring. The principal there, why he taught everything, all those things that I named, he taught all that. They'd have different teachers, you know, in different rooms. A subject here and a different subject in the other room, all like that. But only three subjects that I liked; that was arithmetic, science, and agriculture. The rest of 'em I wasn't too good in.

School wasn't integrated at that time, and I had no problem 'round school except fightin'. Along in those times, people living in town, why they always figger they was better than those people come off a farm. "You just a silly old farmer," that's the way some of 'em felt, like that. The city boys would start to pick at you, saying, "Farm boy!"

The city boys didn't know how old I was. I was small, kinda like a runt, you see. I growed slow, but I was strong. They would ask me sometime, "Hey, little Berry, when you gonna start to grow?!" And so the boys would jump me 'cause I was small. I never started a fight in my life, but I never lost a fight. I whupped everybody jumped me, 'cause see, they was mistaken 'bout my age. And I would whup 'em all, *whupped* 'em, too! Them big boys jump on me, bigger than I was. The girls and everybody 'round there start hollerin', urging the fight on. You know, I didn't want to get in a fight with those big boys. But they picked at me, a country boy. So when one gets on me, I beat him up good. I beat up one of the best fellas they had, and that convinced 'em all! When they got the word, they didn't bother me anymore. All of 'em, they liked me.

They was on my brother Johnny one day. He was younger than me, but he was a little bigger, a little taller, than I was. I was out in the yard, and I heard 'em say, "Hit him!" I looked and they had him up there, 'bout half dozen of 'em. I walked out there and one of 'em had a rock. The leader of the gang was Rab Gainer. He was a fella had a punch mouth, looked like he was mad all the time. He would always start something.

I walked up and he had a rock in his hand. I went out there, knocked the rock outta his hand, grabbed it, and hit him with it. Then all of 'em broke and run, 'cause I had whupped some of the rest of 'em before. They went on. They was 'round there talkin'. Said, "Don't bother that Red. He will getcha!" That's what they'd be talkin' around. "That other one, don't be scared of him. But his brother, that Red, don't bother him or he'll getcha!" They called me Red and my brother was Brown; he had good-looking smooth, brown skin. But they used that Old Red when they talked 'bout me!

Whenever any of us children were going to high school, we stayed in town in Sandersville all week from Monday to Friday. Our house where we lived was out in the country, fifteen miles from school. Right after school every Friday, we would start walking toward home. My father had told us to start walking, and he would meet us in the wagon or buggy. Sure 'nuff, we would start walking, and sometimes we walked seven or eight miles, halfway. We didn't mind walking, didn't worry us at all. We enjoyed that. We continued doing that for three years until we finished high school.

On Sunday evening or Monday morning, my father would take us back to school by horse and buggy. All the time I was in high school I was working. I always kept me a little job working after school. I mostly would work in some of the white people's yards and flower gardens. I made, maybe, forty or fifty cents each day. Some days I made as high as sixty cents.

When I was going to high school in Sandersville, I had a girl friend named Katie Belle, who used to come to town every Friday evening. She was working for some white folks, nursing their babies. The white folks had a home in town, and these people would bring her into town every Friday evening. Sometimes Katie and the white folks she worked for would pass us walking. I was ashamed for her to see me walking. I sure didn't want Katie Belle to meet us that particular evening. Every car we'd see coming, well, we'd think it might be Katie, and we'd dodge outside the road in the bushes.

And so after a while, another car would come along, and we'd think it might be her. Every time we'd see one, we'd dodge, and it wasn't her. Then one time I thought sure it was Katie. I run down through the woods and hid. Then after the car was gone, I come back up. I thought sure Katie Belle had passed by. We all come back up, and then we saw a car coming. We didn't think it was her. That car passed us, and for sure that *was* Katie Belle! We didn't run that time, and she had seen us walking. Later on, when she saw me the next time, she was laughing about it, and my sisters and brothers all laughed and teased me about it. My girl friend had saw me walking from town.

Mama and Papa were never to be outdone. But I tried once, I tried. I was at church, and church was let out. A lotta the school kids and people that I know, they was gonna have a party. Me and Katie Belle was invited to go, and I promised that I would take her. I was going to take her in the horse and buggy; we was supposed to meet up there about six or seven miles from our home.

I asked my father 'bout driving the horse that night. You had to ask for 'em to let you drive. They tell you when you could drive and when you couldn't. And so my father told me, "No, that horse is too tired. You've gotta let her stay in and rest tonight; she gotta plow tomorrow. You'd better let her stay and rest tonight." And so I tell him I ain't going nowhere hardly, just right over here, to so and so. He said, "No, no. You're not used to driving a horse. You got to let 'er rest."

So I went on outta the room. I was mad, but I didn't let him know I was mad. You couldn't let 'em know, you couldn't puff up your mouth or anything like that. So my father and mother wouldn't let me have that horse and buggy. And I wanted it so bad. The other people, I reckon they all went. So that night I was hurt so bad. I couldn't pick up my girl and take her to the party. I was hurting bad.

I noticed some boys 'round the neighborhood had run away from home sometimes. And I hurt so bad I wanted to make Mama and them think I had run away that night. After they wouldn't let me go, I walked out the door and left. I heard my mother telling my father, "Well, Gordy, you should have let Berry have that horse and buggy. Now he done left." I thought she was gonna be worried 'bout me. So I didn't go nowhere but 'round the house. Got by the chimney corner right outside the room where they was sitting and talking. You could hear 'em talking in there, and you could see through the cracks, see 'em. And so I was 'round there listenin'. I thought Mama was gonna argue with him 'bout not letting me have that horse and buggy.

So they sit up there, and they laughed and talked 'bout everything. And this went on. They talked, didn't never call my name, didn't say nothing! I thought they were gonna find out I wasn't in bed or look around. I had just walked on out the door and pulled the door to, and went on out. And I knowed after a while they'd be looking for me. If I'm not there, she gonna think I'd run away.

I stood 'round there waiting for 'em to get in an argument 'bout me. I stood 'round there maybe an hour and a half, maybe two hours, just waiting for 'em. I wanted 'em to say something 'bout me. But they act like they had forgot all 'bout me, wasn't saying nothing 'bout me. I got tired standing up there listening, waiting for 'em to start something. Finally I eased on back, eased through the door, went in, and got in the bed. And so went on to sleep. And that was it! So *I* was outdone that night.

My brothers and sisters, now they had different personalities and different tempers. My oldest brother Sam would fight if he had to fight. He wasn't fussy or a hard fella to get along with. Everybody seemed to like him. Lula was lovely, too. I'd never known them to have any fights, myself. Except her and I used to fight sometimes.

She'd want to try to whup my little fanny sometimes, and I would run. I would be doing something, and she'd get after me, and she couldn't get me to stop. She'd grab at me to whup me, and I'd run. Sometimes I'd pull off a cotton boll and throw it at her. And then she'd break out, try and catch me, try to get me to stop chunkin' at her. I could outrun her, you know. 'Til one day, she kept on when I kept throwin' at her. I fell down, and she caught me by my leg. She grabbed up a piece of cotton stalk or somethin' other and swooped me! I couldn't get loose, and she give me a good whupping. I didn't throw at her anymore after that. But she was all right, she was nice to me. I just messed with her, that's all.

Esther and I got along fine. She was very friendly. She was one of my best-looking sisters. She was friendly and she could laugh. She was good to have fun with, you know. I used to really love her. I don't think we ever had a fight, but she could whup us. She was old enough to whup us smaller children.

Now we get to the next one, Mamie. I was next to her. Course, she wasn't allowed to whup me 'cause we was too close together in age. But her and I were friends, buddies. We was good, we got along fine. She was the one had red hair and was light skinned 'bout my color. Everybody liked her 'round school and everywhere. Everywhere she'd go, people was crazy 'bout her. She was a nice girl, fine.

My sister below me, Lucy, she had very good hair, and everybody told her she was beautiful, and that spoiled her. She didn't study hard at school like my sister Mamie. And she never did get as good an education as we did; she had 'bout the least education. She didn't have as many friends as my other sisters. That's because at school, when the teacher went outta the room and somebody would do something, Lucy'd be the one who'd tell who done it. Nobody else would tell. That made the children not like her, you know. They didn't like her too well. But people made over her so much 'cause of her looks, they'd brag on her, and she'd think she could make it. She was younger than me, I didn't spank her, but we fought. I whupped her a couple of times. My mother would whup us if we'd fight, if she know about it. But we wouldn't tell her.

The next one was Johnny. Him and Lucy got into fights at different times. One fight I remember, we was in the field tending the crop one morning. We left before breakfast, my mother brought out our breakfast to the fields. We was sitting down fixing to eat. Well, her and Brother Johnny got to talking 'bout something. They got to arguing. He said something and all of us laughed. Well Lucy got mad and took her food, throwed it out there in the dirt, just throwed it away. Then she went after Johnny and hit him. She was so mad! Then Johnny grabbed her by the collar with one hand. He held her off 'til he had set his plate out of the way, as far away as he could get it with the other hand. He leaned back and then they fought. Course, he whupped her all right. After the fighting was over, Johnny went back down there and got his plate and ate his breakfast. Lucy didn't have nothing to eat. And we was laughing at her 'cause she was so mad, she'd throwed all her food away.

Johnny would have to be mad to fight. But Joe would fight if you wanted to. He was a good fella, though. Charlie was the youngest; he didn't run with me. He was a happy-go-lucky fella. He didn't work as hard as we did.

I will never forget that last Friday we went home from high school after nearly three years had passed. We walked at least eight miles 'fore my father picked us up. The next morning, which was Saturday, the 31st of May, 1913, we got up early and worked 'til noon. Around noon we all went into the house for lunch.

My mother had the table set with vegetables, nice dinner on the table. We went through the kitchen, and it smelled so good. Well, I wanted to eat so bad, but my father wanted me to come and go over the crops with him. My mother said, "Why don't you all eat dinner 'fore you go?" He said, "No, I'll go now." I wanted to eat, too, but I didn't think no more 'bout eating because my father had asked me to go walk over the crops with him. I hadn't walked over the crops with my father before. And I thought, if he didn't want to eat now, I didn't want to eat, either. If he wanted me to walk over the farm with him, I wanted to do it. So I went on with him.

My father and I started walking over the crops, and he pointed with his hand and said, "This is where Dennis Abron's farm is. This is where his crop starts, from here." And we walked further across and kept walking 'til we got over to another man's crop. He said, "His crop stops right here. Now here's where Johnson's farm starts." We went to some of the other one's crops. He showed me 'bout three or four. We walked 'til we got to his line. And then my father said, "This is where my farm starts, my crop starts right here."

Then he showed me different crops that belonged to different people that lived on our plantation. I had been in school most of the time, and I hadn't never been all over the farm 'fore this. I didn't know where our crops started and stopped. We children had worked on some parts of our farm, but we didn't know where all the rest was. We just knew we was working in the field out there. I knowed the part we was working in was ours, but I didn't know how far out our crop went.

So my father and I walked on. After we got through, we come on back through the plum orchard.

We had a big orchard of plums, peaches, pears, apples, and muscadine arbors. Oh, we had a plenty of fruit on the plantation. Big, long arbors of muscadines. You could smell 'em for a mile. And everything was very nice on the farm.

So after he showed me this, we started on back home. We stopped in the plum orchard and ate some plums for a while. This was very enjoyable, too. We was walking, talking, and eating plums.

After a while a cloud was coming up. It was thundering and lightning. And after a while it got a little closer to us. Papa said, "We better get in, our time is short now." I thought he meant time was short, we couldn't stay out in the weather and eat plums much longer, 'cause time didn't allow for that.

So we stayed out there a little longer. It was thundering and lightning. And then we started back and got to the house. He said, "Yes, well we made it." And so when we got in the house it was thundering outside. I had a letter in my pocket what I had gotten from a girl. I hadn't never read it, hadn't never had the time to open it and read it. And so Papa went in the house and I got my letter and went upstairs and laid across the bed.

It was thundering pretty rough, then. The wind was blowing, lightning was flashing, thundering and lightning. Then after a while I heard a POW; the lightning struck the chimney, and I heard my father holler, and I heard the dog holler. Then I ran down the steps. While running downstairs, I saw my sister and mother

29

and some of the rest of 'em. I asked where was Papa, and they said they didn't know. Then I ran down through the rest of the rooms. We had to go through three or four rooms 'fore you could get to the kitchen. It was a big house.

I ran through all of 'em. I didn't find him down there. I rushed back, come all the way back to the other part of the house and turned and went through another way. By the time I got into the front living room, which was L-shaped, I heard my sister scream. She had walked out on the back porch and jumped back in the door, screaming, "Lord, Papa is dead!" And so we all rushed out there, and sure 'nuff, he was laying flat on his back, just laying there. And so we just knew he was dead. We didn't do nothing. We didn't know nothing to do.

Mama and the rest of 'em was all hollering, hollering and crying. We didn't put our hands on Papa. We just didn't know what to do. They were crying and falling back and crying, "Oh, Lord! Oh, Lord!" That was when I jumped on my horse and rode two miles to my brother's house.

When I jumped off my horse and ran into my oldest brother's house and told him that Papa had been struck by lightning, my brother Sam went to hollering and crying. In just a little while, though, he and his family came up to our big house. After a period of time, everybody arrived at our house. People do not live close in the country like they do in the city. We had to go a long ways to get the doctor, five or six miles. But we finally got a doctor. The doctor come back to our house and examined my father and everything.

The doctor said, "Well, his skin is not broken and he has no broken bones at all. He's not bruised at all." After the doctor got through, he said, "You ought to have just taken him and rolled him over, just rolled him. He would have begun to breathe. The breath was knocked out of him. He was knocked out, he was jarred." The doctor said, "If you had just rolled him over and kinda worked him over, roll him backward and forward, you could have saved him."

Well, we didn't think anything like that. We didn't know what to do, so we didn't do anything. So that's the way it was, the last of it. Everybody hollering, crying. So the next day they came out to make arrangements 'bout the funeral and get my father buried, you know. Things like that. And so I went down to our blacksmith shop.

We had a blacksmith shop, which my father had bought in town. He bought a man out and moved the shop out to our plantation. I used to work in the blacksmith shop and shoe horses. I learned how to shoe horses and fix wagon wheels, buggy wheels, things like that. And I liked to work, weld iron out.

Now I was in the blacksmith shop when the man who was arranging 'bout the burial came in to talk to me. He had been on up to the house, and he couldn't get no understanding of nobody up there. All of 'em was stricken so bad, they were still crying. He said he couldn't get no sense in anybody. He just wanted to know 'bout the burial and everything. So I had to make arrangements of Papa's funeral and burial. I don't know how I did it. But, anyhow, I was the one that taken care of it. I hadn't never cried any.

The cemetery where they buried him was out in the back, in the woods. That's where he was buried at. It was across the hill over there in the thicket, a pine thicket, where the rest of the people was buried. And so they had a grave there. And then they put him in the ground.

There were a lot of colored 'n white people from town there. A lot of white peoples came out there for him—just some of the merchants and different peoples from town. All the family was there, too.

At the cemetery, why, I kinda lost out. That's the only place I felt sorry. After everything was over, when they's letting him down in the grave, when I saw him going down in the grave, then that's the time got me. I was hurtin' so bad I fell down on my knees. I was crawling 'round there like a hog or something. I was bellowing same as a cow. But I was sure 'nuff hurt. I was sure 'nuff crying. I didn't know. My heart felt like it was breaking.

CHAPTER THREE

After the burying was over with, then I had to settle down. Papa owed bills and he owed for this land, and maybe some more debts and things. So I know I had to settle down and take care of his business. We had to have an administrator, we was told, to take care of the creditors that he owed. And we didn't know anything 'bout this.

That's what the white people told us, "Got to get an administrator." So we decided to go down and get one of his friends, Mr. Charley Rollins, the man that ruled the town. He wasn't the mayor, but he was a millionaire, and whatever he said was always done. He owned the property where the jailhouse and the courthouse was. The town rented from him. He owned most everything, ruled the town, and he was my father's friend.

And so, my mother and I, we was on our way down there to get him to be our administrator. So, on our way we stopped to see a white lady friend of my father and mother. My mother told her we was on our way to get somebody to be our administrator.

She asked me who we was gonna get. I said, "Mr. Charley Rollins or some good white man." And she said, "Aunt Lucy, you don't need no white man to be your administrator." She said, "A white man will take all the land you got. You don't need no white man to be your administrator." We didn't know that. And Mama said, "Well, how do you do it?" She said, "Aunt Lucy, all you got to do is go down to the courthouse, to the county building, and tell Mr. Pierce Wood that you want, you and your boy, to be your *own* administrator, and he will tell you what to do."

We went on down to the courthouse, and we explained to him that we wanted to be our own administrator. So he swore us in. We had to put up bond. So me and my mother was administrators. My mother couldn't read or write. She had never learned to read or write, but I was a very good figgerer, and I could read and write. And I was just finishing high school.

You could hear people all around talking 'bout the man is gone, the man is gone. "Old Man Berry is dead." They was thinking we'd never pay for that land now. After they had made me the administrator, the merchants and people come out there trying to sell me all kinds of things. We had never rode in an automobile, we had seen 'em around, but we had never rode in one. A car salesman came out to our house and tried to sell me one. I knew what they were trying to do; get me in debt. Since I was a young man, they thought that I didn't know any better and I would go ahead and buy. This salesman came there wanting to give us a ride, the whole family a ride. When I told him that I wasn't able to buy the car, he says, "You don't have to pay for it now. You go ahead, you don't have to pay nothing, just sign. You don't have to pay a penny now." I told him I got to pay for it sometime. He said, "That will be in the fall, later on. That's several months later." So then I told him that I haven't got the money. The salesman still wanted to take us all for a ride. He had come out to the house along 'bout noon just as we come out from the field. So he give us all a ride 'bout five mile 'round and come back. Oh, we enjoyed the ride so fine. We would have our hand kept out the side of the car and the wind going through your fingers. Oh, we were enjoying the ride so well, and he thought that maybe we were gonna buy it. Well, we got back home, got out and were fixing to eat dinner and then go back to work. He say, "Berry, now what you say 'bout it? You don't have to do nothing but sign the paper. You don't have to pay any money." I said, "Well, I tell you, we're just not able now. I don't want to go in debt like that. We got so much other stuff to pay here, and I don't want to fool around." He said, "You don't have to pay any money at all, just sign the paper." I said, "I'll have to pay for it in the fall." He says, "Well, now, you'll have your cotton all made then, and you won't have any trouble." I told him, "Well, I'm not ready; I just can't buy it now." He talked 'round, but I just wouldn't buy it.

They would come out at different times trying their best to get me to buy just anything, as long as I would be willing to sign "Berry Gordy, Administrator." They told me 'bout some other colored person who lived a little further down in another county, and also 'bout a young man, kinda "pretty good livers," who had bought an automobile. They kept talking 'bout I need one, too. They said people like us should have automobiles. But I wouldn't let no one tell me what I should have, not unless *they* were going to pay for it. So they couldn't sell me a car. Then salesmen came out trying to sell buggies with rubber tires and other things. We didn't buy anything 'til I could see my way clear to pay for it.

Several years back, my father had bought me a law book and told me to read it. He had told me I would need that book sometime. My father was a smart man; I think he was ahead of his time. I had been reading that law book, and I had learned quite a bit about law. I enjoyed reading it, because it had opened my eyes and enlightened me on quite a few things I had run into. But I didn't know anything 'bout an administrator. I don't think I had seen that word in the book before. I didn't remember hearing of it before.

So after they made me the administrator, I knew I really had to take care of the business. I went back home and got my law book and found the chapter where the administrator is. I read that part from *a* to *z*. I read it over and over and over. I really learned what "administrator" means. I learned all of his power and the things you should do and the things you shouldn't do, and I learned how he should handle business. I learned as good as a lawyer or anybody, 'cause I kept reading it over 'til I got the understanding and I know I understood. I knew when to sign administrator and when not to sign administrator behind my name.

The first thing I had to do was to advertise Berry Gordy's estate for one month. Say, "If anybody have any claims against the estate of Berry Gordy, press the claim now or hereafter hold your peace." And then I had to run the notice for four weeks all over the county.

Now, after that, the bills started coming in. I'll talk about four bills that came in. We got one for $400, one for $600, one for $38, and then one for $200. Well, I didn't know he owed those bills.

I didn't think Papa owed those bills 'cause my father used to take me 'round with him all the time when he would go to town. He always took me with him when I was at home. I seen him do business; seen him talk and know where he makes deals at. I 'bout knew who the people were that he was dealing with.

So, after reading in the law book about the administrator and these bills begin to come in, then I went through the receipts. He didn't throw away anything. My mother, she had all the receipts. So I went through all those receipts and found out all of those bills had been paid except one for $38, on which there was a balance due of $6. All of that $38 was paid except $6. And so I had the receipt for the

$32 that had been paid on that debt.

But now we had receipts in full for this $400 and this $600. We didn't have any receipt for the $200, but I stood out that he didn't owe that $200. That claim was from a bank. And so I told my brother Sam that I don't remember Papa borrowing any money from a bank for $200. I don't know that. We couldn't find anything to show he borrowed it, but we found a note and receipt for the rest of those claims. So, anyhow, my older brother said to me, "We better pay that. We can't find a receipt for that, and we just as well pay that." I said, "Well, Sam, I don't think Papa owed that. I don't think so 'cause Papa hadn't borrowed any money. I know 'bout when he borrowed money. I know 'bout those things 'cause he taken me with him most all the time. He didn't borrow money at the bank, I don't believe."

So Sam said, "Anyhow, you better pay for *peace* sake, 'cause you might want to borrow some money sometime, and they might not let you have it." I said, "Well, Sam, I'll tell you one thing. I believe in peace, but I ain't never seen no peace sake worth no two hundred dollars when you don't owe it." He said, "Well, if I had the say-so, I would pay it."

So I went and told my mother what Sam had said. And I said again, "Papa didn't borrow two hundred dollars from the bank. I don't believe that. We don't have a receipt to show he paid it. We don't have anything to show he borrowed money." She said, "Well, if he don't owe it, don't pay it." And so we said we would meet court on that case.

Since we had receipts for repayments of the $600 and the $400 claims, that was proof enough. Therefore, we didn't have to meet court on them. About the $6 due on the $38 claim, we'll discuss that later.

About this $200 what the bank claimed my father owed, well, we went to court. We told the judge we wanted the bank to show proof that my father owed $200. Well, the bank administrator said they didn't have any proofs. "But a man like Uncle Berry, he come in and borrowed two hundred dollars and he was in a hurry and we didn't have time to draw the papers up." The bank man talked on like that, saying they, knowing Uncle Berry was like he was, why, they trusted him. "We let him have the money, but he was supposed to come back and sign these papers," they said. "But he got stricken by sudden death, and he wasn't able to get back and we haven't seen him since."

The judge asked, "This the way you generally do business? Is this your form of doing business?" The bank administrator said, "No, no. This is not our form, but we did it for Uncle Berry." The judge said, "Well, case dismissed." So we won that case.

Now, this other fellow claiming we owed $38 just waited 'til we brought some cotton over to his business place to be baled. Sure 'nuff, he withheld one of our bales of cotton when we went to get it. We was gonna pay him the balance of $6, which my father owed him, but he had had the sheriff to put a notice on the cotton which read that there was a levy on it, and not to move

39

that bale of cotton. We didn't know what to do. I told my mother what had happened, and I told her that my brother and I were on our way to see Mr. Charley Rollins, and she agreed.

My brother and I left and soon arrived at Mr. Rollins' office. I said, "Mr. Rollins, Mr. Frank has one of our bales of cotton and a levy to stop. Mr. Frank claim we owe him thirty-eight dollars, and he's held up one bale of our cotton. But we don't owe him but six dollars." I showed him the receipt with balance due $6. Mr. Rollins picked up his phone, called and said, "Frank, I heard you got one of Berry Gordy's bales of cotton stopped down there. He don't owe you a damn thing! Not a bit more than the man in the moon! You let that cotton alone. Turn that cotton aloose and don't bother Berry's cotton!" Clickup, and he hung up. And so he said, "You go on back and get that cotton." We was gonna pay Mr. Frank the $6, but after Mr. Rollins told him that we didn't owe him a damn thing, we didn't mention that no more.

We then went back home and told my mother 'bout it. And I said, "Mama, Mr. Rollins told us to go on back over there and get that cotton." She said to me, "Well, don't you go over there, Berry. Mr. Frank might jump on you. He might jump on you, so you send Boysie." (Boysie was my younger brother, Charlie.) I said, "Boysie can't load that cotton by himself, Mama. That is five hundred pounds of cotton in that bale." I could do it by standing it up on the end, and then backing the wagon up to it, then push it down and slip it up and slide it on. I could do it 'cause I was strong, but my younger brother was not as strong as I was.

Mama said again, "Mr. Frank might jump on you." I said, "No, Mama. Mr. Frank ain't hardly gonna jump on me." She said, "Oh, you don't know, Berry." I said, "Mama, I tell you, Boysie can't take that cotton; he can't load it. I'm gonna go over there and be just as nice as I can to Mr. Frank. When I drive up there, I'm gonna say, 'Good morning, Mr. Frank. I would like to get my cotton, please, suh.' And I'm gonna be real nice and courteous like. But, Mama, if Mr. Frank jumps on me, I'm gonna do everything I can to hurt him and protect myself." So I just went on and started over there.

So I was riding up on my wagon; my horse pulled up into Mr. Frank's yard. I saw Mr. Frank sitting out on the front porch of the store reading a newspaper that he had in front of his face. He peeked up and saw me driving the wagon. I thought he might take the paper down and say something to me. I got down and walked up. I said, "Good morning, Mr. Frank." He said, "Good morning." But he didn't move the paper. I said, "Mr. Frank, I would like to have the cotton, please, sir." He said, "There it is out there." So I went out there and loaded the cotton and took it back on home. Mr. Frank didn't get out of his seat and didn't take the paper down from in front of his face; didn't say a word. So he didn't get his $6 and so we saved that $6. That's the way things happened along in those times.

Now, one time we had to borrow some money, $500, and they tried to get me to sign "Berry Gordy,

Administrator" and I wouldn't sign administrator. I told 'em no, we was borrowing it from the bank. My mother and my brother Johnny and myself, we borrowed $500 together to help do something to the farm. They said, "Well, you're the administrator, ain't you?" I said, "Yes, but this is not for the estate. This is for three individuals." And so we signed our names individually. They tried to get me to sign, they said it wouldn't make any difference, said it's all the same. I told 'em, well, I knew it wasn't all the same and I wouldn't sign this against the estate. We have to pay this ourselves. Sure 'nuff, that's the way we signed, and they couldn't come back on the estate for nothing if we didn't pay it. They could come back on us only.

I carried the business all the way through like that. I never did buy nothing and let it be charged against the estate. Everything I bought—mules, horses, buggies—everything I bought was as an individual. I never signed nothing against the estate, 'cause if something happened and I couldn't pay it, they could come back on the land; now this way, they could just come back on me for my part.

Now 'bout the property that we have to finish paying off. Papa had taken out a mortgage for $1300 on the 100 acres of land where we lived in the big house, in order to buy 120 acres of land about two miles down the road where my oldest brother Sam and his family lived. The 120 acres was the last piece of property that my father bought. Since we still owed $500 on the big house, we now owed the bank $1800 all total. So, after we had gotten over the shock of Papa's sudden death and got things straight around the house, and straightened out all the notes, we started to work hard to keep the farm going and to pay off the property.

CHAPTER FOUR

We had a neighbor down the road who was an old white man they called Old Man Ennis. He was a tough old man. He didn't like my father 'cause my father moved off the plantation when he bought it. Old Man Ennis bought it off a man by the name of Mr. Sweeny. Now my daddy was renting from Mr. Sweeny, but he moved when Mr. Ennis bought it 'cause they had such a bad name. Well, Mr. Ennis had six brothers. They all had killed somebody. Nobody knowed how many people Old Man Ennis had killed. Ennis had money, and people was scared of the Ennises 'cause they were bad folks with whiskey stills in the swamp. Those Ennis brothers were bad folks! The revenue agents or the sheriff would go to the Ennis place and find a still in the swamp and take it out. Mr. Ennis would send word for 'em to put that still back down there. He'd do all that kinda stuff. They would carry the still back. The revenue agents and the sheriff were scared of those Ennis people. They was white, but they was bad folks, and the people in town were afraid of 'em.

Now, the colored folks that worked for the Ennises wanted to be bad. People called the colored folks that worked for Ennis those Ennis niggers. They tried to be bad like their old white boss. Their boss would whup 'em 'round. The Ennis niggers would whup up other colored folks, but they didn't bother white folks.

If the Ennis niggers get in trouble, Mr. Ennis would go down to the jail and pay his niggers out. He'd let 'em work for him and just keep 'em like slaves. Mr. Ennis didn't pay 'em nothing as I know, but he'd work 'em and feed 'em and clothe 'em. They tried to be bad like their boss. The boss could kick 'em around and whup 'em, and they wouldn't do nothing. Now, when they get 'round the church, 'round colored folks, they'd be tough. They'd shoot 'round the church, and beat up and shoot up colored people. And so that's the kinda people those Ennis niggers were.

My father and his friends built that church, and he was the head man in the church. This was a Methodist church. It was called Cabin Hill. The Ennis niggers come 'round there cussing, and my father would have 'em prosecuted. He would have 'em taken to court. Old Mr. Ennis would come 'round there and pay the fine. Whatever it was, he'd pay. He'd take 'em on back to his plantation and work 'em. He'd keep 'em there and feed 'em and work 'em and boss 'em and kick 'em around like they were children. He would work 'em at the sawmill and on the farm.

They was crazy 'bout him, and they'd take his kicking 'em around. We've seen him whup them old, big black men that worked on his plantation. He'd walk up to any one of those men and hit him and knock him down; they'd hit the ground pleading and crying, "Oh, Cap'n boss," just like a baby. They wouldn't do nothing, wouldn't fight back at all! As soon as they get 'round the church, they'd have everybody scared of 'em. Ennis niggers was bad!

This big fella, Marshall Gary, was mad with us 'cause my father had him prosecuted. He weighed over two-hundred pounds and was 'bout thirty. One day we went up to Mr. Ennis' to pick cotton for Old Man Sammie. See, after we'd get through picking our own cotton, we'd go out and pick for other people. We'd pick 'bout a bale a day sometimes, and maybe more. Oh, we'd make 'bout fifteen dollars for a bale or something like that. Sometimes make twenty dollars a day with our crowd. We could really pick cotton. A bale of cotton weighs five hundred pounds. There was 'bout eight of us. We'd pick 'bout one hundred pounds apiece.

This particular day we went up there and this old fella, who Papa had prosecuted, saw my horse and he knew the horse. While we was picking cotton, he come there and just started whupping my horse. He took his old, long whip and just hemmed my horse up in the fence and whup him 'til he just cut the skin off of him.

We wasn't there. We didn't know nothing 'bout it at the time.

When we stopped to eat dinner and started up toward the house, we looked and saw my horse standing in the corner just a-trembling. He had long scars, his hair was cut off, his skin was cut off. I was so mad! I told my brother Joe and my brother Johnny, I said, "Somebody been whupping my horse!" and I was nearly 'bout to cry. I said, "Whoever whupped that horse, we gonna whup him!" I didn't care whether it was a white man or a colored, we meant to whup him! Me and my brothers filled our pockets with rocks to fight with.

There was a big crowd of men, nearly 'bout twenty-five or thirty just standing 'round. Mr. Ennis had a lot of 'em working at the sawmills as well as on his farm. Some of 'em were down on the ground shooting dice. They were all around and I walked 'round and I'd say to different groups, "You know who whupped my horse? Ya'all know who whupped my horse?" They said, "Naw, naw, we don't know nothing 'bout it." Then I'd ask another bunch up there, "Do ya'all know who whupped my horse?" They says, "Naw, we don't know." One fella said, "Maybe you should ask the fella out there." This old big guy laying out there in the sun with his hat over his face and a whip laying 'cross his breast.

I walked over there and I said, "Marshall, you know who whupped my horse?" He went to getting up, then. He stood up and said, "I hit her a lick or two." I says, "Well, what you hit her for?" He said, "Well, she

47

was in my way and I had to get her out the way." I said, "You didn't have to hit that horse to get her out your way." I said, "Next time you do that, I'm gonna do so and so," and I said, "Mr. Harper Tucker, the overseer, told me to put that horse in there." I said, "I asked Mr. Tucker could I put my horse in the lot and he said yes when I first got here."

Marshall said, "I don't care who told you to put her in there. If Mr. Tucker told you to put her in there or Mr. Ennis told you to put her in there or if God told you to put her in there and she be in my way, I'm gonna whup her damn ass."

When he said that, I hit him, and I was so mad, I hit him with a rock—*a-bam!*—and he hit me with his whip. It wrapped all around and tied into my neck. I reached up and caught it with my left hand, and by that time Joe done hit him, Johnny done hit him with the bricks—*bam, bam, bam, bam.* Marshall whirled, broke and run, and the whip come a-loose from 'round my neck. I got in behind him. I outran and caught him and grabbed him in back of his overall suspenders. He whirled 'round and grabbed me and slammed me down on the ground; and while I was on the ground, he was trying to get a chance to hit me, and I was reaching up and tying my hand up in the whip, and he was trying to get away and hit me with the staff of the whip. I was reaching up, and while I was doing that, Johnny run there and grabbed him by both his legs making him fall over. By the time he hit the ground, Brother Joe had a piece of two-by-four. He hit him right in his head—

a-bam—right in his forehead, and knocked him down. He raised his head up and Joe hit him again. Marshall cried out, "Come here, somebody. Come here!" By that time, Brother Joe hit him again. He fell down and his mouth went in the dirt and I was getting back so Joe could hit him again. I wanted him to hit him another lick! Then Marshall fell down and didn't say nothing. He just laid there. Joe hit him so hard that time 'til he broke the two-by-four, and it flew 'round and hit me and cut the blood outta my ear.

I was gonna let Joe hit Marshall about six more times, and then we would have him 'bout whupped. By that time, some other men had run over and had us all. One had me and one had Johnny and one had Brother Joe. They was pulling us away. They was all saying, "That's enough, boy. That's enough!" They took Marshall up and carried him up in the kitchen. They rubbed him with camphor and stuff. They was working on him, just rubbing. He was just down and out. Just out! We didn't know we had him that nigh dead.

So we went on back to work that afternoon. That evening, 'bout four or five hours later, we saw some of 'em Ennis niggers coming along in this timber cart. At that time we was hitching up our horse to go home, and so they passed the road where we was supposed to enter 'fore we got down there. This made us be riding behind 'em. We wanted to pass 'em, but we didn't know if they was gonna hit us when we passed, or what they was gonna do. We wanted to get a chance to shoot by 'em in a hurry in our buggy. But they slowed up and we was kinda slowing up, too. Then we saw 'em stop and act like they was working on their cart. So we stopped and was just sitting in the buggy. I told my brothers, "I'm watching back here, ya'all be ready, 'cause there is no telling what they gonna try and do."

While I was talking to my brothers, that same old Marshall Gary got his stick and 'fore we knowed anything, he come running back! All three of us were sitting in the buggy together. Here he come, all two-hundred-odd pounds, running. I jumped out on the other side. I run 'round the buggy, reaching for the rocks in my pockets. While we was getting our rocks out, Johnny, who had jumped out on the other side, had got his rock. When Marshall passed the buggy to come 'round in behind me, Brother John saw him coming 'round the buggy 'bout to hit me with a big stick. Johnny throwed a rock right 'cross that buggy and hit him above his ear. Marshall kept running straight down the road, right on down to the branch. We were shooting him with rocks. We were hitting him with rocks just like somebody shooting. He was running so fast, he ran way down to the branch. He didn't stop; he didn't have time to stop. We come back and got in our buggy.

I was mad! I run and got in the buggy and run up to my uncle's house 'bout a mile further up the road. I told his wife, Cousin Jenny Johnson, I said, "Cousin Jenny, I want to borrow your gun. It's some birds down here, some partridges, a drove of partridges down here. I want to kill some of 'em." She said all right and gave me the gun. I wanted 'bout two or three more shells. It was a double-barrel shotgun! I ran back outside there and jumped in my buggy. I turned the buggy 'round and down the road we was going to meet the Ennis people near Mr. Davis' house.

When the Ennis people had got near 'bout to Mr. Davis' house, they saw us coming in the buggy. I had that horse trotting. I was going to shoot 'em as soon as I got there.

Aunt Martha Spanks saw us coming. She jumped out in the road and run up to the buggy with both hands up in the air, and she was hollering, "Stop! Stop! Stop!" Aunt Martha Spanks is an old lady like my mother. My mother and Mrs. Spanks was good friends. She knew us well. She was hollering, "Stop, stop! Don't do that; don't do that! Stop, Berry, stop!"

We always obeyed and listened to old people whenever they tell us anything. Sure 'nuff, I stopped and she said, "Turn that horse 'round and go on right back up that road. Turn that horse 'round!" Sure 'nuff, we turned on 'round and carried the gun back. We gave it back to Cousin Jenny. That was the end of that part of it! After that incident, Marshall never did bother us anymore, himself.

After we got home, all the town peoples were talking 'bout our fight with the Ennis niggers. They all were laughing 'bout it. They were talking 'bout how we beat him up. Everybody was talking 'bout those little knee-pants boys—how we beat up that big man. Everybody heard 'bout it. He was one of those bad Ennis niggers, and we like to have killed him! Now we wore knee pants even until our twenties. But 'cause we all had on knee pants, they named us the "knee-pants boys." And so, from then on, all the town folks know we would fight if we had to.

CHAPTER FIVE

The people in town there, in Georgia, well, they thought very nice of us Gordys. They used to call us "big dogs." But now, I don't think they use that name anymore. They call 'em "big shots." But they used to call 'em, long in those days, "big dogs."

Everybody, all the girls 'round there I know, respected us very highly. I'll tell you the truth. I was a young fella, about twenty years old, 'fore I started dating. In fact, I was 'round twenty years old when I was still wearing knee pants! The old people wouldn't let you wear long pants too soon 'cause it makes you think you are a man too quick. You wouldn't be grown 'til you get twenty-one. When you get to twenty-one, you call yourself a man. Long as you was down below that, why, you wasn't a man.

So I was about twenty years old when I started

dating. But, of course, I had girl friends when I was a little younger. After we got to be young men, while we were in our teens, well, we had to be home 'fore sundown. Like we go to church on a Sunday, we'd have to be home 'fore sundown, when it got dark. We'd leave our girl friends and come home 'fore dark.

I didn't bring my girl friends home to meet my mother, particularly, but the girls would come home with my sisters just to visit 'em sometimes. And while they were there, they would meet her. But I didn't never take girl friends to let my mother meet 'em. . . . I was ashamed. They never kissed me with my mother 'round. Sometimes, I'd be around church talking to a girl, and just 'fore my mother come, I'd kinda quiet up and wait 'til she'd pass by, 'round the church, you know. I was ashamed for my mother to see me trying to "court," you know, or something like that. I guess I might not be aggressive, but then, I could have a lotta fun after my mother's gone! I wasn't scared of girls at all, though. No, I wasn't scared of the girls. I like the girls pretty well, I was wide open. Yeah, I like 'em, but me, I was a little runt that the girls didn't like; I learned that early! But I was wide open, *then.* Course I hadn't met my wife, yet. And so, I know my way 'round pretty well.

Well, I didn't date too many girls. I had 'bout three good girl friends, just 'bout three is all I had. Outta those three was supposed to be 'bout the best girls 'round anywhere. Two of 'em was from "big dog" families like us Gordys, the other one wasn't. One of 'em was just a nice girl. She worked for white folks, nursed the babies. And her mother and 'em didn't have nothing. But she was all right. She was a good-looking, intelligent girl; but was too poor to be the best girl around.

But there's a lotta girls I would have fun with. I talked with 'em, I was nice to 'em. Some I'd take to church sometime. They'd know my sister or something like that. But I just didn't like 'em for girl friends, but I'd be nice to 'em.

One day I visited school where my sister taught. It was in town, about fifteen miles from my home. Course, I went to that school myself. They had an exhibition with all the teachers from the different counties all come together with the principals of the schools.

I walked into there and my sister met me at the door and kissed me. And she told me, she says, "I want you to meet the little Fuller girl here. She got the first prize." I said okay. I walked up there, and she had her back turned to us, doin' something. And so my sister said, "Miss Fuller, I want you to meet my brother." She swirled around on her heels, and we met each other. And I looked at her, and she was cute-lookin'. I said to myself—I didn't tell her—"That's my wife!" I stopped by to see her on my way out; talked with her, then. And sure 'nuff, I got a date at her home. I had never met her before, and got her address and everything, got a date for another time!

So I saw her later on. She was sent out to my old elementary school to teach. So she wouldn't, she couldn't get away then! Course, she had some nice boyfriends. I didn't know I had competition, but I had a little. She had a fella had much more to show than I did. The guy was six feet tall, fine-lookin' guy. He had a Buick car. But I didn't never worry 'bout it 'cause I didn't never have any trouble with the girls. Whenever you get popular with two, three of the best-lookin', best-rated girls, you know, everybody admires it. Why, you have no more trouble. They thought I was from a good family. I always kept the old people thinkin' that I was very religious or a very good boy. Well, in fact, they thought all the Gordy boys were good, yeah. The old people trusted me anywhere with their girls. I even helped some of my friends steal their girls. The girl's parents didn't mind me takin' her out, but the families didn't like the other boy. So I'd take her out for a ride, and the boy would meet her when I carried her 'cross the river. And the parents would trust me.

So then, after I had met the girl who I knew was gonna be my wife, I had to go to the service. I got drafted! Yeah, and that's one reason I hated bad to go in the service. Thought I might go over there and get killed! Hadn't of got married, yet! I had a good-looking girl friend. I had two, three of 'em, good-looking girl friends. I wasn't worried about my girl not waiting 'til I get back, no. I thought I might get over there and I get killed and I ain't never been *married*! I just wanted to get married 'fore I die. My parents was strict on us, you know. And you didn't know much 'bout girls! And I wanted to get married 'fore I *die*! And I was thinkin' at the time, when we go over there, we go to fighting right away. I didn't know they gonna have to go through such long training, and all like that. I thought they gonna get you lined up and fixed up and give you a gun. My mother, she didn't want me to go. She cried, she prayed, she didn't want me to go to the army to fight. And I didn't want to go. But it wasn't I was too scared to go. If I had to fight, well, I could fight. But I didn't want to go 'cause we were still trying to pay off the property.

If they take me away from here, if they have no administrator here, there's nobody to manage it. The white people want it already, and I know they would take the property. That's the other reason I didn't want to stay in the army. I had to get back to try and get that debt paid up. And I did everything I could to get out of it.

But in the army, you didn't have to go out and fight right away; you have a long time 'fore you get on the battlefield. You have to go through a lotta things. We'd take hikes, twenty-mile hikes. Go all through the woods, jumping over logs, 'cross creeks and things. There's where you get your training, march, drilling practice, and everything. But I always was sorry in those things. I'd try not to best 'em. I did everything I could to get out of it. I went there tryin' to get out, all the time. That's the first thing that I tried to fail at. I tried my best to fail in the army, not make a good soldier. But I wanted to do it in a nice way. I didn't boast about it. I was humble as a lamb, and tried to do what they tell me to do. But I acted dumb! I couldn't learn nothing!

I couldn't learn how to 'bout-face, or right face, left face, color right, or color left. I couldn't learn none of those things, I'd mess up every time. They took me outta the line one day and try to let me practice in front of the whole line. Say, "Come out here. Right face!" I'd act like I was jumpin'; make a figure. He says, "No, turn on the right heel! Right face! Turn on your right heel and your left toe! Tuck your feet together!" I'd go, I'd turn it, and then I'd jump on it. I'd make a mess of it. He tried maybe a half dozen tries, try to get me to do some of it right. And I'd miss it. Then he said, "Well, get back in line!" I said, "Wait, give me another chance!" I act like I wanted to learn. And he'd give me another chance. I tried, I'd miss again. He put me back in the line. And so I was no good at that.

The camp I was in was Camp Gordon. Then we left there for Newport Hill, Virginia. That's where I stayed. And all the time I was there, I was trying to do something to get out. But I didn't want 'em to think I was trying to get out. I stayed sick there. In the mornin' I'd be in the sick line. At first, I was a cripple 'round there; leg, hip, everything hurtin'. They couldn't find nothing wrong with me, but I still hopped. I know they couldn't tell, but I was afraid they would. I hopped on a stick down there for a long time, and they thought I was crippled. They let me police and clean up the grounds there. See, you have a stick with a nail in the end of it, and just go 'round clean the yards up, just stick that paper with the stick. That was my job.

I'd hop around, hop around all day long like that.

So one day, a half a dozen of us went to the post office at noon to send off a letter. We thought we'd run down and come back 'fore they called us out to drill. So I think I was the last one finished with my letter. I got through and mailed my letter. I looked out the door and saw these other four, five fellas was strung out a-runnin' up the hill there to get in line to be drilled. Then I looked and saw the whole platoon lined up there. All of 'em! They out there, lined up, ready to drill. And these fellas runnin' ahead of me had got there, and I run behind.

I knew I was late to drill, so I wouldn't go to the end where the officer was. I went across to the other end of the line. I thought I'd get in the line on the far end, and he wouldn't know who I was. But when I ran across there, the officer hollered at me, and I act like I didn't hear. I got in line; thought I was safe. He started to hollerin', "Fall out! Fall out!" And then started pointin' at fellas, "You, you, you!" So I got outta line, and he had me come down there and he lined us all up. I was worried 'bout that, didn't know if they gonna court-martial or shoot us, or what. I'd seen 'em punish some of 'em with a water hose bigger than the fire department's. That's a lotta water that's turned on by the barrels full. A man, about two hundred fifty pounds maybe, put you under there. He held your one arm and another held this one, and they'd just hold 'em under there and let the water come. I seen 'em do a fella like that one time. I sure would hate to go through that.

But when he got through drillin' us late ones, he

59

had something like a baseball diamond, and had us all to line up around that diamond. I didn't know what he was gonna do. He put one of us here, one there, one there, all 'round. He said, "Now, the men that get caught are gonna be punished. But if you catch a man, you go free." He shot a little gun for us to start. I went to hoppin'. I was hoppin', hoppin', hoppin'. And I looked back, I see this guy reaching at my back. So, I put both feet down, I went to runnin', I caught my man. But he didn't get me, though! I had to stop that hoppin'!! They all laughed so hard. It was funny how that ole cripple learned how to run! They have a big laugh, and he didn't do nothing else to us 'cause they had so much fun from it. They find out I wasn't crippled 'cause I was runnin' too well. I had to cut that hoppin' out!

Well, I got to study something else, now. So I'd be back in the sick line every mornin'. So one time the doctor come there. He examined me, couldn't find nothing wrong. So the doctor told me, said, "Are you here again?! Your head should be shot off your shoulders." Well, I just mumbled. I just lookin' like a lamb, just quiet. And then, he got this inoculation, what they stick you with. He just stuck me like he's mad with me. And it hurt! They'd stick this medicine or something in you, to make you be healthy or something. He went on with the next one down the line.

They'd have me lay in quarters 'stead of goin' to drill. As I told you, I was sick all the time; something wrong with me. And they'd have me to get the sick list for everybody. Every mornin' I go 'round to the barracks; write down everybody there who was sick. I'd write their name and line 'em up, take 'em to the hospital 'cross the hill there. Well, I'd get all the names written up, but then when I have to call 'em, some of the names I could pronounce and some I couldn't. And I'm the one that had written 'em! But I get some names I can't understand. I half called it something else, and it wasn't right. They had to help me read my own writing!

I did all those kinda things, trying my best to get back home so I could take care of that property. 'Cause I know the white people'd take that property. And I'd do anything, but I tried to do it in a nice way, without gettin' 'em mad or something like that. They thought I was just a poor fella, poor fella, never learn. And so I went along with that for a while. I got to where I made out like I couldn't see. I couldn't read good, my right eye was kinda blind.

And so the last day they took me on a truck up to some place where they could examine my eyes. They told me to go on down there and pass the first two doors, turn to your right at the third door. Between the third and the second door, you had to go through a little place there with not much light. It's kinda dark, shadowy, in there where there wasn't much light. When I walked through that door, something like a little needle jumped up in front of my face. I ducked under it, you see. It might have been a rubber needle, I don't know what. But when I got there, I saw I was gonna walk right in, and it was gonna stick my face; I ducked my head down under it. You see, I saw that needle in the dark! The doctor had me come back, so that didn't work.

Anyhow, I couldn't do nothin' too good. Well, I'd always try. Least I had 'em thinkin' I was doin' the best I can. And finally, I knew something. They was figgerin' sending us all overseas. But they didn't have my name in there on the list! Some of 'em find that out before I did. They come to me cryin', wanted to know why I wasn't goin'. And they come to me, cryin', ask me to tell 'em how to help 'em get out. I wouldn't say nothing; I was glad my name wasn't on that list. I hadn't got out yet, and I didn't want to talk 'bout it then. I'd say, "I don't know, I don't know." They'd say I'm not goin'. But I didn't know for sure. So two, three days later, they give me some papers to take up to the quarters somewhere over there in Virginia.

So I went there. I gave the papers to a man, he opened 'em up. Then, the man gave me seventy-five dollars cash money and gave me back these papers. Say, "Well, now, you take care of those papers. They're worth thousands and thousands of dollars to you. That's your discharge." That's what he said, my discharge! I wouldn't laugh at all. I looked just as solemn as I could. I didn't make any different; he said it's my discharge! And I was so glad!!! He said to take care of 'em, and I said, "Yes, sir." And so, I asked him what train to take back to Georgia. And he told me where. I didn't go back to the barracks and get nothin' I had left there; clothes, shavin's or anything I had left there. I went straight on into Georgia on the train and went on along to my home. They was glad to see me. Mama and all of 'em in the family. They said they'd prayed me home. "Callin' on Jesus can do 'bout anything," Mama said.

No, I didn't spend over three months in the army, 'cause I was too dumb. I couldn't learn nothin'! Yeah, and so when I got back home, I had an honorable discharge on disability! He said I got the best you can get. But there was nothin' wrong with me! I did everything, but about being dumb, you can't hurt nobody by being dumb! They don't put nobody in jail for being dumb!

And so, when I got back, the big people in town there, they know I had no right to be back, much as they know 'bout me. The education I had in high school there, and the name I had... they all knowed me. And you know, they came out there. Police came out to see me. Detectives came out to my house and wanted to see my discharge. Well, I was scared to show it to 'em, 'cause I thought they might take it, keep it, and I wouldn't have one. And I told 'em, well, I couldn't show it to 'em. They said, "That's what you got it for, to prove that you didn't run away. You have to have something to show, that's what you got." Then I thought it over. I said, "Well, I'll tell you. I'll show it to the judge, in the courthouse." I wouldn't mind taking it to the judge in the courthouse, let him know 'bout it. But I wouldn't give it to those detectives. I didn't know what they might do. They might've tried to keep it, and then they'd have to fight me. I wasn't gonna show it to 'em. But they agreed with me to take it to court.

So I had to go down to the court. And when they called my case, I walked up there. I hand the clerk the discharge, and he read it. And somebody else read it. And they let the policemen see it. They say yes, he's got it. So there was nothin' they could do.

Now that I was outta the army and everything was settled, I went back to work then. They had raised a lotta cotton; it was a good year. And it was a good price for cotton that year.

We handled the crop ourselves, we didn't have to hire nobody. After we finished our own crop, we had time to go out and work for other people and make some extra money for ourselves. We'd go 'round to different places and work after we get all our cotton in. When I was in the army, I'd get letters from home 'bout the price and the height of the cotton. I told 'em to hold it 'til they can get top price for it. So they held it 'til I got out. I got out sooner than they thought. I thought to get out later on, but I got outta there when cotton was high.

We had two wagons and had stacked 'em up with a bale here, a bale there, I don't know how many bales. But the wagons were sure 'nuff full. I went down to Sandersville, sold it all, and paid for all of that land—everything! And I didn't spend no money for anything except paying the food debt. That way, I knowed we'd be safe. And after then, I begin to buy things what we could pay for, you know. So we came out all right.

CHAPTER SIX

I t was 'bout maybe a year after I got outta the army
that I thought I'd get married. I wanted to get
married 'cause I didn't know what's gonna happen
to me. I went to see Bertha Fuller, my girl friend. If I
didn't get her, I had another girl friend. But she's the
one I liked best. And I asked her 'bout, if we got married, what would she have to do and all that. She said
she had nothing to do. She already got everything! And
I got ready for her.

Now, proposing to her, well, I talked to her like I'm
talking to you now. We agreed on these things. I guess
I didn't really propose or whatever, except to ask her
if she agreed to be married. We agreed on it, that was
it. I don't believe, back then, I knew what was the
routine you had to go through with. If I had knowed it,
I might have did it. But course, I just talked with her,

she agreed, and that was all it took.

Anyhow, her and I started to get married after we talked to our parents and everything. I wasn't too nervous 'bout talkin' to her parents. 'Cause I know if they wouldn't give her to me, I was gonna steal her; that's what I had in mind to do. I had that much faith in myself that I could steal her if they wouldn't give her to me 'cause that's what I wanted. And I'd known of some who stole their wives.

So, anyway, they talked awhile, talked awhile. They didn't want us to marry at all! Then, they wanted us to wait some time, 'til school's over, maybe. They give us thirty days; we could get married in a month. At first, I wasn't gonna wait the time. That was when school would close. Then I got to studyin' 'bout it.

She was teachin' school down there at Mount Pleasant. I would pass along there and see her every day. I got to studyin' 'bout they give me a month to marry. If I couldn't be seein' her every day, well, maybe I could have waited a month. But then, I thought, yeah, we could get married anytime. So I talked to her and we decided to get married the next week! And, sure 'nuff, we told 'em 'bout it, gonna get married the next week. Well, they didn't kick on it. We went ahead and, sure 'nuff, got married the next Sunday.

We didn't have a big wedding. We just had a certain amount of friends, 'cause it takes too much time to get a big wedding. Never did have jitters or nothin' like that like some of the bridegrooms have. I never was scared 'bout it. Whatever I wanted to do, long as I thought I was right, I wouldn't be scared. Hadn't never done it before, but I wasn't scared. I might get a little bit nervous, but I wasn't really scared. After the wedding, we went by another friend of ours that got married the same day. We spend a few minutes with 'em, then went home. Yeah, I brought Bertha right back to the house.

I didn't have mother-in-law troubles, either. I've heard people talk 'bout their mothers-in-law. But my mother-in-law was crazy 'bout me. She was a principal at the high school. She was as nice as she could be. I loved her and my father-in-law the same way. He owned a racetrack. They was crazy 'bout me, and I was crazy 'bout them. We didn't have no trouble at all.

And so my mother was agreeable 'bout me and Bertha bein' married; she was agreeable. My brothers and sisters were married, too. Now, when my older brother Sam got married, my parents were agreeable for his marriage. He got a girl that they loved, a nice girl. But when my older sister Lula got married, they wasn't in for that. They didn't want her to marry him.

Well, one thing 'bout it, he made a lotta money; a good, fast talker. My father and 'em didn't think he was the type for our sister. And at the time, I was younger, I just agreed with what my parents say. Now since I grew up and know what kinda fella he was, he wasn't the type for her. But still she loved him. They talked against her marryin' him, and see, that's one thing you'll find: When the parents talk against a fella, the girl gets more crazy 'bout him. I've seen that now many times.

If you don't want the fella, brag on him! It's better for you to brag on him in front of the girl. If she's thinkin' of marryin' and so you take to speakin' of "Oh, he's so wonderful!" sometimes she begins to wonder what you gonna say 'bout her. She might feel, he should be glad to get *her*!

So it's a bad thing when you talk against the fella. The more you talk against him, the more she might feel sorry for him. But my parents were right 'bout him. He was smart talkin', fast talkin', and made money. But anyhow, they got married.

My second sister Esther married a well-to-do man, too. But he was a very smart businessman, good farmer. He was older than her. He had a good living and was crazy 'bout her. He had lost his wife a couple of years before. They didn't kick 'bout him 'cause they knew he could take care of her. He was all right, he's just a little older. At those times, they didn't want you to be too much older. But now, it doesn't matter. But they liked him.

My sister Mamie got married after my father died, but my mother didn't kick 'bout her marriage. But she died in childbirth. My youngest sister Lucy got married 'fore her, though. Course they all got married 'fore I did. My father was living at the time Lula, Esther, and Lucy were married, but he passed 'fore the rest of us were married off. With the last sister's marriage, the fella didn't ask me for her hand. He just told us they were gonna get married. We didn't say nothin'. Course, he was a good friend of mine. So she liked him, he liked her; I didn't kick. They didn't come ask me to give her up, they just got married!

I was a person always liked a lotta fun. I used to tell a lotta jokes, you know, keep the gang laughin' tellin' jokes. My wife was a very intelligent girl, smart. Like I said, my wife was teachin' school. I'd tell a joke and have people laughin' all the time. She kinda broke me from that, kinda made me more intelligent. She would say, "You always got some foolishness going on." I'd say, "Well, people enjoy that, havin' fun, everybody enjoyin' themselves." Yeah, but she wanted me to think 'bout more educational things, or somethin' or other.

Berry Gordy, Sr., in the 1940's. ▷

Opening day of the Booker T. Washington Grocery Store in Detroit. Pop Gordy is standing on the right, holding turkey.

△
Berry Gordy, Sr.,
in uniform about
1917.

Bertha Fuller Gordy, age 16.

Lucy Hellum Gordy, Pop Gordy's mother, outside family home in Sandersville, Georgia.

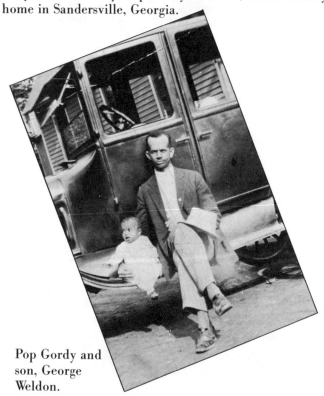

Pop Gordy and son, George Weldon.

Pop Gordy built this house in Sandersville, Georgia, in 1917 for his new bride Bertha and himself.

Roosevelt Street in Detroit where Berry and Bertha lived during the 1920's and 1930's.

Bertha and Berry Gordy in 1923.

Bertha and Berry Gordy in 1970.

Pop Gordy (far right) joins the B.G.'s Top Ten baseball team.
Family members starting in the back row, left to right: Robert
Gordy, Jr. (Robert L. Gordy's son and Pop's grandson); fourth
from left, Berry Gordy, Jr. (Pop's son); Kerry Gordy (Berry,
Jr.'s son); Robert L. Gordy (Pop's son); Berry Gordy IV (Berry,
Jr.'s son). Middle row, second from right: Terry Gordy (Berry,
Jr.'s son). Front row, left to right: Glenn Gordy Fuqua
(Gwendolyn Gordy Fuqua's son and Pop's grandson); Kennedy
Gordy (Berry, Jr.'s son); Derrick Gordy Fuller (Pop's
grandnephew).

The Gordy family at home in their apartment over the
Booker T. Washington Grocery Store. From left to right:
Berry, Jr., Loucye, Gwendolyn, Anna, Esther, Bertha and
Berry, Sr., Mrs. Marie Boddie (friend of family), Grandma
Lucy Hellum Gordy, Evelyn Turk (cousin residing with
family), Fuller, George, and Robert.

Pop Gordy addresses a church
group in Los Angeles.

Shown with Pop are members of the cast of
The Wiz, during filming in New York City.
Michael Jackson is on the right.

CHAPTER SEVEN

When the cold weather come, white people would have a lotta hogs to kill. They would hire a lotta colored people to come 'round and help kill the hogs every year. The colored help would work all day. Some would be pullin' hair off hogs, scaldin' 'em, and some would be rippin' 'em open and takin' out the insides. Others would be over at a big long table workin' with the insides called "chitlins." They would be dumpin' 'em out and cleanin' 'em and turnin' 'em over. Some would be cuttin' the heads off the hogs and puttin' 'em in a pot and boilin' and cookin' 'em. Some would be makin' lard and doin' all different things, workin' all day.

Then at night when the colored people get ready to go home, the white people didn't pay 'em any money; they'd just give 'em a hog head, some chitlins, and the

78

hog feet—things like that. That's all they'd get; they didn't get no backbones or spareribs or shoulders or hams or sides. They didn't get none of the good parts of the hog. They'd get chitlins, hog heads and hog feet, tails, and things like that. That's all they'd get, and they would be perfectly satisfied. They didn't worry, they'd be happy.

The white people had told the colored people 'round there, and our foreparents, that on the first day of the year, January first, if you have a hog head and black-eye peas on New Year's Day, you gonna have good luck all that year. Colored people believed those things! They were happy to get those hog heads and didn't worry about nothin' else. Now, the first of the year, they would always cook black-eye peas and hog heads and have a ball!

But you go 'round the white people's house on Thanksgiving Day or New Year's Day, and they have all the turkey, ham, and different things, good food. They didn't have any hog heads 'round; in fact, they gave 'em all away. The colored people were glad to get 'em. And it went on like that for years and years. Some of 'em is still that same way, now. Every New Year's Day, they have hog heads and black-eye peas and they believe those things the white man told 'em and they never learned any better. I laugh 'bout it sometimes. I say poor people, some of 'em will never learn. Course, what you're raised up doin' all your life and whatever you grow up believin', if you don't begin to think for yourself, you will continue to believe it all through life.

'Round the time I was twenty-eight or so, I began to sell fresh beef with a meat wagon I owned. On Saturdays when the folks were gettin' paid off, I'd sell to 'em. I'd be parked with my meat wagon at one place, and this white man would be parked at another. There would be a lotta people standin' 'round my wagon just waitin' for me to cut their beef. I'd holler out, "Fresh beef, fresh beef!" After I would holler, "Fresh beef!" the white man who was standin' off a little distance would say, "Fresh beef, fresh beef . . . nice and clean under the screen and *no flies*!"

After a while, I'd holler out again, "Fresh beef, fresh beef!" The people still continued comin' out, standin' 'round me. They knew I had good beef. So he'd holler out again, "Fresh, fresh beef! Nice and clean under the screen and *no flies*!" I laughed. It didn't worry me 'cause I knew I had me the best beef. I didn't know what kinda beef he had, but I knew I had nice steer beef. I only kept 'bout eight head on my farm for myself, so I would go out around the neighborhood to find people who wanted to sell a steer. I'd buy the steers and bring 'em home and butcher 'em. I'd kill one or two every Friday. I just had my business. I made good money. I'd sell out all my beef way ahead of him, and I'd leave. Many times the people would tell me that the white man would get there ahead of me and tell 'em that I wasn't comin'. But they said they knew I was comin'. I'd say, "Oh, yeah, I'm comin' every Saturday." They just wouldn't buy from that man, they would wait 'til I come. I had a real, real good business.

I was independent. I had plenty to eat and always had money. I had so many hogs and I had so many acres of land, so I built a pig pasture and I built a lane that come right up to my barn. I made a big mud hole there for the hogs just to waddle in. Then in the pasture, I had a couple of mud holes out 'round the spring where they could waddle in there and cool off. So, when I go outdoors and holler, all of those hogs would start up to the house. When they'd get to the lane, they would get close together and just line that lane from one end to the other, there were so many. I don't know how many head of hogs I had. I just had eight head of cows, but a hundred or more head of hogs.

The pig truck would come through the county and want to buy some pigs. I'd stop there and I'd sell 'em 'bout fifty dollars' worth of pigs and I wouldn't miss 'em; I had so many. Fifty dollars along in those days was some money. It was good money! Sometimes, I'd sell a hundred dollars' worth like that!

Anyway, I was just independent even in those days. I thought to myself, it doesn't make sense to spend your time makin' somethin' that you can't use yourself, like cotton. In which case, you just got to wait on the other fella and be dependent on him. But as long as you got a-plenty to eat and then make somethin' that everybody has to have, even the president of the United States got to eat to live, then you're doin' somethin'. I could demand the price of my food 'cause people have to have food. If one won't give me the price, I can sell it to someone else.

The last few years that I was in the South, I didn't plant one seed of cotton. I had nothin' but peanuts and things to eat. I raised cattle, hogs, chickens, and all those kinda things. You can make an independent livin' growin' things like that. One thing the white man know is the way to handle people is to keep 'em hungry, keep 'em beggin'. Then they can handle 'em just like they want to. That's one thing we got to think 'bout in life. We got to try to arrange to get outta some of these ruts we're in. There are so many things in life that we colored folks miss the boat on.

So I was independent in those days. My wife helped me, though. Oh, yeah, she helped out on the farm. She picked cotton. Even when she was pregnant, she worked, helped me out. She had to go home from pickin' cotton one day. She left the field to bring the first child, my oldest son. She was workin' up 'til the last day.

Now, when I begin to be a father, well, I felt very happy; I was happy every time. I was always hopin' for a boy somehow or other. I don't know, for a fact, what Bertha was hopin' for. But when the girls come, I was just as happy; no difference. 'Bout naming 'em, I just left it up to my wife. Whatever she wanted to name 'em was all right. But I wanted the first girl named Esther. I had a sister, Esther, that I loved; the sister whose house I used to stop at. That's the only one that I picked out the name for, then I let my wife do it. She named my first boy, that's Fuller. Now, Fuller is her family's name. So then, she give him part of my name.

His name is Fuller B. Gordy; *B* meanin' Berry. But they never called him that, just straight Fuller B. I didn't like that name, Fuller Berry Gordy, I would rather have it just Berry Gordy. Course, I didn't worry 'bout it too much. I don't know why, but she named the seventh one Berry Gordy; we had eight children altogether. But I was glad for a Berry Gordy, yeah.

I kinda give things over to her, let her do whatever she's satisfied with. Like I 'fore said, we had eight children. The first three was born in Georgia. We had four boys and four girls; a perfect match, fifty-fifty. Course, we thought after we had six, that was gonna be all; that's what Bertha said. And I thought since that's what she say, maybe it would be so. But then, the last two of 'em come, too. That was all right with me, though. Now, I can give you all the children's names: the boys are Fuller B., George, Berry, and Robert, and the girls are Esther, Anna, Loucye, and Gwendolyn.

Like I 'fore said, I had vegetables; I could go down and sell a load of greens and different things. I'd go down, sell beef, and like that. We'd go into town and just sell stuff: watermelons, chickens, vegetables, all of that. The Negroes could do that: sellin'. We had no trouble sellin' things we had. There's some white people in those quarters that had big firms, big sawmill. But we could sell.

I always had money; I had money all the time. So I had in mind to open up my own store. I was lookin' to do big business 'cause I had a lotta things goin'. I was growin' in my business, and I was lookin' to have a big market where I could sell these stuffs I had. I already had a little beef market of my own, my meat wagon, and now I wanted a big market to run my own business and sell out to the people all 'round there. I had a big mind to do it.

Then I sold a bunch of timber stumps from our land for my mother and 'em; sold it for two thousand six hundred dollars. I got a check for it on 'bout Tuesday. That's two thousand six hundred dollars! If a colored man in the South there had that kinda money, well everybody likes to talk him outta it. White people and everybody say, "This Negro has two thousand six hundred dollars!" There was different people I'd talk with. This doctor, a white doctor, asked me when am I gonna cash this check. I told him I didn't know. Well, he said he'd take me down to the bank where I could put it in a safe bank. Fact was I already know of a safe bank to put it in; the bank that my father used 'fore he passed. I wanted to put it in there. But he wanted to go down there to help me deposit it at the bank. And not only him, but also another white fella! He wanted to go and "help me." I didn't need no help. I could put the money in the bank myself!

Course, I knew the people, the bankers, the people that owned the bank. I'd worked for these people in town around after school. So I didn't want to let these peoples who wanted to help me know when I was goin' to the bank. When they come to see us they'd say, "Well, I'm going downtown. Come along, I'll take you on down, and we'll get your check cashed," and so and so. I told my mother and sister 'bout it, and they didn't want me to fool with these people.

I was at church on Sunday, and my sister told me that day that my brother John was leavin' for Detroit. She said it would be a good idea for me to go there. Well, I had no idea of goin' to Detroit. I was gonna farm, get my business goin' just like I wanted. So she said, "Those white people is so interested by that check. I think you should go on to Detroit and get the check cashed up there. You fool 'round here, they're liable to beat us out of it, take all our money." I didn't think so, but she kept on encouraging me to go. 'Bout an hour after John left for Detroit, she was still talkin' to me. He went there to live, but I hadn't thought 'bout goin' to live there, myself. But they kept on after me like that, so I decided to go. I didn't know that when I left home on that Sunday mornin' to go to church, I'd wind up goin' to Detroit. I was talked into goin' and I left; I didn't even go back home, I just left.

The train had gone already, but my father-in-law said he would take me to Milledgeville to catch the *Shoofly*, a little short line train. Then, I could go across and catch the Central to Macon and then catch the train to Detroit. I agreed on it, and so he took me there. I caught the *Shoofly*, but when I got to Macon there, the other train was gone. So I had to wait for the next train goin' to Detroit; I caught that one. So I got to Detroit 'bout four hours after my brother.

CHAPTER EIGHT

I got up there in Detroit and I saw how things was. I saw a lotta people makin' money. But I wasn't makin' money! I just kept lookin' 'round to make money. But I liked it so well; I knew if other people were makin' good money, I was gonna be able to make some. I was reading the paper and it say where the plumbers were making twelve dollars a day, and the bricklayers and plasterers, too. I could get a job in a blacksmith's shop paying four dollars and a half a day. Well, that's more than I ever made in a regular job during off season down in Georgia. Down there when the crop was in and it was wintertime and all, I'd get jobs for a month or two and they didn't ever pay over two dollars a day.

So I just know I could make big money in Detroit. I wrote for my wife, Bertha, to come up; I was gonna stay here. I told her to sell out everything. I meant for her to sell the cows, our home, the chickens, mules, horse, wagon, and buggy, sell everything! But she didn't sell nothin'!! I was lonely, you know. I kept writin', forcin' her to come on up. It was only a month 'fore I could get her here, but it seemed to me like six months! I was so anxious for her to leave Georgia, and I didn't give up on that. So Bertha came to Detroit, bringing our little children with her. She left all the cows, mules, the home, and everything. Everything was left there in Georgia. Then I begin to struggle up here in Detroit. We had some hungry days now, off and on. I struggled on and I kept on scufflin' 'til I got goin' where I could kinda make money.

When I first come to Detroit, I asked somebody where was the best side of town for colored people. Somebody told me the west side. But at that time, my brother was here livin' on the east side. Before my wife and children came, I stayed there at my brother's house. Then when they all got here, I rented a place for three or four months.

Now that I was in Detroit, I had to get me a job. I heard that the Michigan Central was hiring. And so I went there and I got a job as a blacksmith. They was payin' seventy cents an hour then, and so I was glad to work there as a blacksmith.

The men were picketin' the front gate there, 'cause they had a strike on, but I didn't know it. Some of 'em told me 'fore I left work, don't go out by myself 'cause the strikers was out there and they'd beat me up. I

didn't know 'fore that nothin' 'bout a strike bein' on.
The job was easy to get, but that's why I got it so easy,
'cause they wanted help. I was "scabbing," but didn't
know it. And so I was scared to leave. I stood 'round
there, I didn't know anybody. When the cars would go
out, they'd be loaded down, five or six men in a car, and
the pickets didn't bother 'em. The car would go through
there, shoot out on by 'em, and no attack was made on
'em. But now me goin' out by myself was a little different. The pickets had whupped up some people the day
before, that's what some of the people told me. I didn't
know what in the world to do; I didn't know how to get
out!

So I watched all the cars as they begin to leave.
The last car came out. I didn't know those fellas, but
when they passed by me, I jumped through their window, over in the laps of those people that was in that
car. I didn't know 'em, and they didn't know me, but
when I jumped in there, fell on top of their knees, I was
gonna take a chance on 'em whuppin' me. I didn't want
that mob to get me out there. I just fell over there, and
so they didn't do anything; they let me ride on up there
near Dix Highway. When they got up there, they put
me out. They said, "Well, you're out of danger, now."

Now, I saw two fellas comin' towards me. They
happened to be picketers. They saw me get out of the
car; they stopped me and asked me 'bout workin' over
there. I told 'em, "Yeah, I come out from over there
workin'." And they said, "That's why we got the trouble we have now. We're picketing that place for more

money, and by you coming in there working, we can't get it." And I told 'em, "I didn't know that you was strikin'. If I had, I would've never went there." I talked to 'em, begged 'em, and so they didn't bother me. I asked 'em if I could go back and get my money, and so they told me I could go back and get my money the next day. I went back, and when I got there that mornin', oh, they had a long table, and all kinda nice food on there. I was hungry, and I thought I'd go in and eat breakfast. I hadn't meant to do nothin' but get my money and leave there and not work. But I saw this food, it looked so good, and I was hungry. So I sat down and had breakfast like I was goin' to work, too. And after I ate, I was ashamed to walk out and not work that day. So I went on to work, takin' another chance to work that day.

I know I had to get out again that day, and I had to take the same chance that they gonna beat me this time. I got to thinkin' 'bout they gonna beat me up good, or somethin' like that. But I made arrangements with some of the rest of the men 'fore they got out, to go out with 'em. So I had the luck to get out. I got my money, and I told 'em that I couldn't come back. So now I had to go somewhere else and get a job.

I found a couple of little, small jobs somewhere else, but I didn't like 'em 'cause they wasn't payin' enough. I wanted some bigger money. So I went searchin' for "big money." I looked in the papers and saw where they payin' plasterers so much, and I always want some of that big money. So I went to a place; I just walked 'round. I saw the people plasterin' overhead ceilings. It looked like they was doin' it so easy, so easy. I just know I could do that. So I asked 'bout workin'. They told me no, they didn't need any help.

Then, I went to another place. I just knew I could plaster, 'cause it looked so easily done. I asked the man about did he need any help. He said, "Yes, you a plasterer?" I said, "That's right." He said, "Where's your tools?" I said, "I didn't bring 'em today; I'll bring 'em tomorrow. I just come out to get the job. I'll bring my tools tomorrow." So I had in mind to go out and buy some tools. He said, "Well, I have a kit of tools inside there; you can use my tools." Well, the man knew at that time I was no plasterer by the way I spoke 'bout it. He could tell, but I didn't know he knew. I thought I could plaster. So I went in there; I didn't know what to get outta his kit. I looked at the tools, then I looked over and saw that they had a hawk and a trowel. I got the same kinda lookin' tools that the other men had.

Now I didn't know how to get the mortar off the table. They just come in and scoop it up so easy. But I couldn't do it; I didn't know how to do it. I had my hawk down side of the table and took my trowel and raked some of the mud off and let it fall on my hawk. I was watchin' the other men outta the corner of my eye, 'cause I was so awkward with it. I saw 'em lookin' at me cross-eyed. So, I got my hawk full of mud, and I see 'em pitchin' up and cuttin' under it, then throw it on the wall so easy. I went to throw some up and cut it off like they was cuttin' it; all that mud fell on my bosom and it hit the floor. I looked 'round to see who was lookin', and I saw this fella winkin' his eyes at this other fella. They was laughin', turned their heads around laughin'! I was so nervous.

So I raked the mud up and put it back on my hawk, then I leaned up close to the wall. I took up some on my hawk and tried to rub it on the side of the wall; it all fell off again! The boss was peekin' through the crack at me, 'cause he knew I wasn't a plasterer to start with. But I thought I could make it. He come to the door where I could see him. He didn't say nothin' to me. With his finger, he beckoned me to come to him. I went to him, and he said, "I can't use you." I was so glad the man told me that. The trouble now was, I was so shame! I wanted to get outta his sight so bad, I wanted to run! But I just walked on out; I wouldn't look back at him. I was so *outdone.* I got behind a bush where they couldn't see me, and talkin' 'bout runnin'!! I made it to the streetcar line and I went *home*! I got enough of tellin' people I could plaster.

I found another contractor, a colored contractor, by the name of Ralph Gailliard. I told him I wanted to learn how to plaster, be an apprentice. He told me, "Well, now what you'll have to do, you'll have to learn how to make mortar first, and then as you learn, I'll get you a hawk and trowel." He made me a little wooden hawk and bought a trowel. I had to cut fifteen bags of mortar. He showed me how to chop that mortar. Fifteen hundred-pound bags of mortar; hard wall. And I had to cut it and put it up on the board there for the other two plasterers. I had to learn to do it the hard way.

The mortar makers, at that time, were makin' eight dollars a day, and the plasterers were makin' twelve dollars a day. Well, I had to do that eight-dollar job for two dollars a day! Mr. Gailliard said he can pay me two dollars a day and teach me how to plaster and make mortar. And so I was satisfied to take that job like that, 'cause I was so anxious to learn.

Now, I'd come home late at night, and I'd leave home about seven o'clock in the mornin'. I'd get to the job about seven-thirty A.M., start cuttin' my mortar, and 'bout eight o'clock I'd have a batch of mortar ready for those plasterers soon as they get there, undress, and get ready. I'd cut all day like that 'til late, five or six o'clock in the evenin'. And my wife, she went along with my workin' those long hours. I didn't worry 'bout the long hours, 'cause I was so anxious to learn this trade. I knew if I learned this trade, I could make twelve dollars a day; I wasn't worried. So I went on for quite a while. And on Saturdays, when they paid me, why I'd come home with twelve dollars for all the week. My wife say, "That's all you got?" I told her yes. She said, "Why don't you get another job?" I told her, "I want to learn this trade." So, I stuck with it 'til I thought I had the job down. I stuck with 'em 'til I thought I was doin' pretty well.

After I learned what I could, I left those people that I was workin' for. I had some tough times, though.

I'd taken some jobs I thought that I could do. But I messed up some of 'em. I didn't know I had messed 'em up, and some of those people I did the work for didn't know, either. I continued on like that 'til I got to where I was better and better. Finally, I got so good, 'til I did get a job with some people who were good plasterers. I had a time tryin' to keep up with 'em, but I tried. They hired me in the union. I wasn't a good plasterer. I could put it on, but I couldn't straighten it up like the rest of 'em. But I kept on like that. Then, I got a job with some other people.

The plasterer was a very nice fella by the name of Warren, a white fella. I was workin' with him, and he would help me with the things I couldn't do too good; he would straighten it up for me. He had a colored laborer there, but that laborer there gave me the hardest way to go. He was worried 'cause they was payin' me the same as this white fella, and I wasn't as good. The colored man talked 'bout it, but the white fella didn't bother and wasn't sayin' anything 'bout it. This colored fella was named Charlie, and he'd make me pretty mad. He didn't like it 'cause I was gettin' all that money! He kept on sayin' that I wasn't as good as him, and I didn't want him to be talkin' 'bout that 'round the boss.

Then the boss came 'round one day. I was anxious to make a good showin'. They had the planks wide apart and this other fella could just step and he'd never miss a plank. But I was tryin' to keep up with him to make a good showin' to the boss. I missed the plank and fell on the floor! The boss didn't say nothin'. But this col-

93

ored fella, Charlie, he was laughin' and said, "I swear, he calls himself a plasterer and can't stay on the scaffold!" He just kept a-talkin'; I was so mad with him. The boss still didn't say nothin'.

So that evening the boss told me to meet him at the bar tomorrow mornin'. And sure 'nuff, I met him at the bar. Then he paid me off after we got to the car line and said that he wouldn't be needin' me on the other job anymore. So that was the end of that job.

CHAPTER NINE

L ike I 'fore said, I was renting a place on the east side, but a fella told me the west side was the best for colored people. So I went over there huntin' for a house to rent. I saw a real estate man, and he said, "What you want to rent for, why don't you buy a house?" Said he had a house up here that's nice and clean; newly decorated. He said, "The amazing thing about it is, you can move in right now; as soon as you make the deal you can move in it." He said, "You might go somewhere to rent a house, and the people will still be in there. It takes some time, but I can sell you a house and you can move in it right now." I said, "Well, how much is it?" He told me eight thousand five hundred dollars. I said, "Eight thousand five hundred dollars! I don't have that much money." He said, "Well, you just pay a down payment on it, and you can pay it by the month, 'til you get it paid off."

Now I knew 'bout buying land down South, but I had never bought any house property, and I didn't understand how to go 'bout gettin' it. Anyhow, the real estate man guided me along. He said, "Well, I have somebody who wants the property, but if you want it, I'll let you have it." He asked me how much I had to pay down on it. I told him I couldn't pay over $250 down. See, when I cashed that $2600 check for the timber, we split it up amongst the family and I didn't get to keep but $250. "Well, I can arrange that," the man said. "You give me that two hundred fifty dollars to put on the down payment. The rest of the down payment would be my commission anyway, so I'll loan you my commission. Then you can pay me back by the month at the same time you pay your house notes. We can work it like that," he said.

He took me over to see the house that night. He turned the lights on and all the floors were just glitterin'. The new wallpaper on the walls looked so nice, and I liked it so well! He said, "Well, what 'bout it?" I said, "Well, I don't know, I don't know." I wouldn't give a direct answer. He said, "Well, if you don't want it, somebody else wants it, but I thought I would help you out. You could move in tomorrow, soon as you make a deal." This was on a Saturday. He said, "Come over here at ten o'clock in the morning, and we'll run out to the landlady's and we'll see 'bout the deal." Sure 'nuff, he picked me up in his car, and I was there on time that next mornin'. He said, "I got to rush, we got to be

96

there at eleven o'clock." I had decided that I wanted
to take the house, but I wanted to talk with the landlady. The real estate man kept rushin'. He kept sayin',
"Got to be there at eleven o'clock. The landlady said be
there at eleven o'clock."

When we got there, we went into the landlady's
house and spoke to her. The real estate man introduced
me to her by sayin', "Miss so-and-so"—I can't recall
her name, now—"this is Mr. Gordy. He wants to buy
the house." By that time, the phone rang. She answered
it, "Mr. Singleton, it's for you." He went to the phone
and said, "Oh, I'm sorry, I have someone here to buy
the house, now. . . . I don't know. . . ." So he kept on
a-talkin'. "Well, if he doesn't take it, I can let you have
it. . . . Well, I don't know, I don't know. I was looking
for you, but you didn't show up. Now, this man wants
it, so I had to come on." And he kept on, "I don't think
it would be fair for me to let you have it when he's
already out here and he wants to buy it."

I was listenin' at the real estate man, like he was
changin' and might let somebody else have the house.
I was just worried. He went on with his telephone con-
versation, sayin', "No, no, now if you were here and
another customer called in and wanted to buy the house
that you wanted, you wouldn't want me to turn you
down for him, would you? You've got to think about
that." He said, "Well, I'll tell you, if he doesn't buy it,
I'll call you right back, and you can come on out and
get it." He closed by sayin', "All right, okay."

Mr. Singleton come right to me and said, "Well,

Mr. Gordy, what do you say?" I said, "I'll take it, I'll take it!!" I was scared; I was glad he didn't let the other fella have it. Now that was a trick he pulled on me. The real estate man had somebody to call him soon as he got to the landlady's house.

That's why he was rushin' so hard to be at the landlady's house at eleven o'clock. They called him right at eleven, too. Now he had me thinkin' somebody else wanted to buy the house. Naturally, I jumped at it; I bought it. Sure 'nuff, I paid the two hundred fifty dollars down on it, and then I was goin' to pay 'im so much a month along with the notes. I was workin' night and day. So I went on and paid the house note and the real estate man every month. I went on like that for a number of years. I soon paid 'im off his commission, and then I had just the notes to pay. I went along payin' those notes year after year, year after year.

I'd worked so hard at plastering and such that I put a little money aside and bought me a grocery store over on the east side. I just worked hard, kept on and worked very hard. When Mr. Singleton sold me the house, it had new wallpaper on and was freshly painted. Soon after we moved in there, the children hit on the walls, and the paper would burst, and the old plaster would fall out. It wasn't nothin'!! He papered over old plaster, and I had to replaster that house all inside. The kitchen ceiling was 'bout to fall out, too. But when I bought the house, it was painted and decorated so nice. I didn't know too much 'bout houses. I didn't know how to examine the walls and things, so I had a lotta violations. I had to do the plasterin' inside and a lotta other work.

I went on paying off the house. 'Bout that time, the city inspector come 'round. They condemned the plumbing, condemned everything there. The city inspector told me it would take three thousand and some odd dollars for me to fix the house up. Three thousand and some odd dollars, and I didn't owe but two thousand eight hundred dollars in payin' for the whole house! I just got to studyin' on it. I thought, if I put three thousand dollars more on that house with the two thousand eight hundred that already was, well that's gonna make 'bout five thousand eight hundred dollars in all. And I'll be 'bout where I first started; just an old frame of a house. I figured if I put that kinda money in it, and when I finish it's still gonna be just an old frame of a house, that isn't gonna be worth much to me.

So I told my wife 'bout it and what it would cost to get it back where it would pass inspection for the city. I said, "I don't think it's wise to fix it up, 'cause it ain't never gonna be worth too much. Here's what we'll do, we'll just save up all the money we can make and don't pay anymore on this house. We'll stay here as long as we can, 'til we're put out. Maybe we can save two, three, or four months or whatever amount of time he let us stay here. We just don't pay him, just tell him we haven't got the money and stay here and save money as long as we can."

Sure 'nuff, we stayed at 5419 Roosevelt for three or four months, and we saved our money. Just before we finally had to leave, my wife and I and our eight children moved into a house on Hudson Street with her sister, brother-in-law, and their eleven children. A year or so later I rented us a house on Stanley Street near Olympia Stadium, but we soon moved outta there 'cause we found out a man named McCann had murdered his wife and cut up her body in that house. I'd found a building on the east side which cost the same as the house that I had on the west side. It was run down but I had got to where I could do the kinda work to fix it up. So even though we lost that little frame house on the west side, we now had a nice brick building which had living quarters over the store.

There were more people and more business on the east side. Like I 'fore said, I'd already bought a grocery store over on the east side, but I didn't own the building it was in. Now the building I just bought was just one block from it, and a little later on, I moved the grocery store into our own building. We had a big grocery store, we sold everything. Everything was stocked in the store: meats, bread, milk, just whatever a good grocery store has. We had the nicest store of any colored anywhere in the city. Nicer than a lotta white folks'. We had a nice setup there. And we named it the Booker T. Washington Grocery Store.

We lived there in that neighborhood from then on; for thirty years we lived right there in that place. Everybody knew us, liked us fine over there. It just seemed like a better neighborhood; had some very nice people but some rough people, too. We never had any trouble about people breakin' in or robbin' our house, but we got stuck up at the grocery store one time.

I had just hired a girl to be a clerk that mornin'.

People was in the store tradin' and all. This fella come in, and he asked her 'bout a bar of soap. She went over to get it, got the bar of soap, and brought it back to him there. I was standin' there with seventy-four dollars in my hip pocket. And so I heard him say somethin' to the girl. I looked 'round, and she looked at me. He stuck up the girl first, and when I looked, he turned to me and pulled the gun on me! He said, "Give me all the money you got! Give me all the money you got and put it in a bag!" I said, "Uh. . .what?" He said, "This is a stick-up!!" I said, "Oh, oh, I didn't understand. Oh, I don't mind givin' you the money. You come a little too early, though."

I was a-talkin' all the time I was goin' to the cash register. I said, "You come too early. The lady hasn't got here with the money, yet. We ain't got no money, yet." And so, I just hit the cash-register drawer. "I got fifty cents in here; it's all we got, now," I told him. "Course, if you'd waited, you could have got more money." And I give the money to him. He said, "You son of a bitch! Turn your back!" I looked at him kinda cross-eyed. Well, I wanted to do what he said, 'cause I didn't think he was gonna shoot me or nothin'. So I just kinda turned 'round. He backed on out the front door with the fifty cents, and he broke and run. He come right down the side of my store; through my glass windows, I could see him a-runnin'.

Now, when I had my grocery store, that was just a side thing. My business was plastering and carpentering, doin' that kinda work. I did all that work all at the same time. I'd go to the marketplace early, five o'clock in the mornin', and buy fresh vegetables and things for the store. I'd bring 'em back and then start my own business by seven o'clock in the mornin'. I'd do my plastering and carpentering work 'til late at night, come home late, and keep a-doin' that day in and day out, day after day, day after day.

I'd be runnin' my business, and my wife would take care of the store. And the children, when they come out of school, they'd help in the store. Oh, yeah, I kept my grocery store all the time I raised my children, and I put 'em all to work in there. We started 'em workin' there when they couldn't even see over the counter! You could go in there and see the little children there makin' change. People couldn't understand how they could make that change so well. It was 'cause they was all smart! And we showed 'em all how, put 'em to work!

I guess I followed in my parents' footsteps 'bout bein' strict on the children. But I always thought 'bout what to be strict on. I tried to figure it out, what I thought was best. Me and my wife, we was very strict on our children 'bout school. They had to go to school, they couldn't stay home. We was strict on 'em doin' their work at school and homework. If their marks wasn't good on their report cards, we talked to 'em 'bout it. We wanted 'em to bring in better marks, and so they brought in pretty fair marks like that.

When it come time to punish 'em, well, I'd find out all about it. If they done somethin' wrong, I'd tell 'em what they done, tell 'em. I would take a switch to 'em, a strap, or somethin' or other. If they'd disobey, give 'em a good whuppin'. The girls, too! I whupped the girls, too. But I didn't have to whup 'em much. I'll tell you, if you start off children when they're young, you whup 'em just a few times when they're young, they'll get a understandin' that you mean what you say. You have to mean what you say when you're a parent. You ain't gonna have too much trouble with 'em if you raise 'em like that.

One thing 'bout it, never whup a child unless he's wrong. When you whup him, he don't like it at the time. But when you get through whuppin' him, stop hurtin' him, he knows he was wrong. He won't hate you for it. Parents shouldn't come home half drunk, treat the children bad, get angry or rough, and fight the children jus' 'cause they in that condition. It's accordin' to how you carry yourself. The things that their parents do, what they teach 'em ... well, the children gonna be somethin' like their parents. You got to do your best to raise the children right and start 'em in time. You just start 'em off early, you won't have any trouble.

Another thing, I never bothered with the children when they were fightin'. Long as they fight a person the same size, I let 'em fight; fight their way out. That way they will know what they can do. If you run in there and take up for 'em, stop 'em, that's no good. Let 'em fight; they'll make friends afterwards, sure. We never had to go and get after nobody 'bout fightin' our children, either. Course, we didn't encourage 'em to start no fight.

If we find out they started it, why, we'd get after 'em 'bout it. But we always told 'em, don't bother nobody unless they jump on you! We taught 'em like that. So we never had to go and bother nobody 'bout our children fightin'.

I used to go to church regular; still do go regular. And I always took the children to church with me and my wife. I had a little trouble with 'em goin' to church, just like my parents use to have trouble with me; same thing. But they had to get up, you know. You wake 'em up. . . . They just hate to get up.

When children spend a lot of time in church, they get tired, mischievous. But you have to train 'em to sit there. Every once in a while, why they might want some water. So, I'd give 'em some water. Then, they want to go to the toilet; we'd take 'em there. Sometimes I had three or four of 'em, a little baby on one arm, one in the other arm, and the rest of 'em followin' along. I didn't mind doin' it, it wasn't nothin' to me. Sometimes I knowed they didn't need to go, they just wanted to get up. But we didn't have too much trouble keepin' them quiet in church, 'cause they were trained.

I used to be a trustee in the church, helped 'em organize; never overloaded myself. My wife Bertha started the Sunshine Band there in the Church of God in Christ. She had a gang of small children 'bout eight to ten years old or maybe twelve. Course, she'd been handling children in school, you know, so she had the experience. She liked it, and she did a good job with the children in church.

But now 'bout the children and workin', I worked 'em when they were young. I fed 'em and clothed 'em and give 'em money; what money they needed. I didn't consider that I had to pay 'em like you pay any outsider. Never did feel like I had to pay 'em, 'cause I'm gonna take care of 'em and buy everything they need. Send 'em to school and do everything. That's how my parents did for me.

With the store, we didn't never completely feel our grocery bill. We had plenty to eat all the time. We just go into the store and get it. We didn't keep account on it and all like that. My specials to eat were greens, black-eye peas, pork chops, bacon, sweet potatoes, milk, biscuits, syrup, and butter. Those things I give mention to, that's soul food. But I like steaks and things like that, too. We had it all in our store.

Later on I wanted to sell the store 'cause my other work was good, and I just didn't have time to run to the marketplace and buy stuffs for our store all the time. I kept on after my wife Bertha 'til we agreed to sell it. But we continued to trade with those people that we sold it to. We still had to eat, so course I'd buy from 'em.

So I told my wife to keep account to see how much it would take to feed all of us. So she kept account of it. The first week, when she found out how much it was costin' us to live on groceries, it was so much!! Then I told her, "Well, you don't have to keep account of it." It was so much more than I expected. So I said, "I don't want to know. Just go ahead and eat . . . eat . . . eat!! Just buy and pay for it!"

My plastering and carpentering business was good. When I had some time, I'd take the family, we'd go to the parks and things like that. We'd have footraces and things 'round the park on certain days; holidays and different things. We'd play ball, just go take the children. We'd take 'em over to Belle Isle Park and different places. Belle Isle had a beach, so we took 'em over there. Sometimes, we'd go to the movie show, but we didn't bother 'bout movies long in those times much. We were just scufflin', tryin' to make a good livin'.

My wife and I, we'd go to some dances some. I didn't dance much in those days. I wasn't thinkin' I was a professional, either! But some of 'em said I'm a good dancer. Course, all you got to do is get out there. Just do any awkward step you make, keep time with the music. I don't care what you're doin', someone's gonna think it's a new dance, and say, "Oh, you're wonderful!" I'd cut so many different steps. Sometimes I'd get my legs tangled up, and everybody fell in and started to do it, too. They'd think that's a new dance step! They don't know. You can make a dance up of your own; any kinda thing that you do, someone will see you, and they'll try it. You can clown. . . . In fact, good music can make you cut some good steps! If you got a lotta life in you, the better the music is, the better you can dance! I didn't keep up with the bands in those days, though. The only band name I can recall is the Jimmy Wilkin Band.

CHAPTER TEN

After I left the South, I thought when I got North to Detroit, the people would be altogether different from the people in the southern states. I thought they were better with everybody. I heard people speak so well of the North. But when I got up here, I found out it's just as bad here as it was in the South. It's so many things here. . . . Every violation, every law or rule they make, it hits the colored man or the poor man 'fore it hits anybody else. The rich and white folks can get away with things, but the colored man and the poor man couldn't get away with nothin'! In everything, the colored and the poor have to live up to all the laws and toe the line on everything.

I remember when I was workin' for this plastering company, and I became a contractor. I got me a good gang of plasterers and then I happened to get with

Brownwell Corporation. Now, Brownwell had an inspector. This inspector would come 'round every week and inspect my job. And every week, he would hold up from fifty to seventy-five dollars on my paycheck. He would point out a little somethin' wrong with the work, a crooked angle that was off just a fraction; just any little thing. But he'd name somethin' that usually wouldn't take me over thirty minutes to fix it. But every week fifty or seventy-five dollars had been held back on my check. I would just try to make my work perfect. I thought he was doin' everybody like that. So I went on for such a long time like that. Every week I tried to improve my work, but every week still, he'd hold back fifty or seventy-five dollars.

I went 'round and checked some of the rest of the contractors' work, and I found out that their work wasn't nothin' like as good as mine. So the next time the inspector come 'round my job, I told him I had checked some of the rest of the jobs and the jobs wasn't nearly as good as mine. He said, "Never mind 'bout the other people's work; you get yours right." I knew he was right about that; it was right for me to do my work right regardless of others. So I checked closer behind my men, 'cause I wanted 'em to do everything perfect. So that week I inspected every job. I went from one job to the other to see if my men were doin' everything perfect, 'cause I didn't want the man holdin' no more money out of my pay; I had to pay my people off every week. I paid my plasterers good money, and sometimes when I paid off, they would have more money than I would! So I didn't want the inspector holdin' nothin' back, 'cause I needed all my money.

In spite of all my good checkin' that week, he held back fifty dollars. I flew hot, then! I went down to the Brownwell Corporation office and told the president about the job over there on Griggs and Grand River that we had just finished and how the inspector come there and held back fifty dollars on that house and that I didn't see nothin' wrong with it. I asked him to come over and check it, and the president said he would be over there on Sunday at eleven o'clock. Sure 'nuff, Sunday at a quarter to eleven, I was there, and I waited for him. When the president got there, as soon as he stepped inside, he started smilin'. He looked all over the house, looked at all the walls, ceilings, and all around the grounds and everywhere. Then he went into the closets and looked. If you're gonna do any bad work in a house, you're gonna go in dark places; a closet or back somewhere where you can't see too well. He went in those two closets, turned his back to the angle, and rubbed his hand up and down the angle. It was just as slick and smooth and troweled out, just as neat and nice. So he walked out and said, "Well, all right, you come down Monday." I said, "How do it look to you?" He said, "It looks good to me. You come down Monday and get your money." I said, "All right, thanks."

I went down there Monday and sure 'nuff, when I got there, he give me my money. I saw the inspector 'round there, and I didn't say nothin' to him. The president didn't mention the inspector to me. But anyhow, that inspector, he got fired! The president didn't tell me he was gonna fire him, but he fired him, right away. I was doin' good work and the inspector was takin' advantage of me and the president found it out. Mr. Harry Durbin, he's the man; he was the president. He's the man that fired the inspector. Mr. Durbin use to be the housing commissioner of Detroit. He was the president of the Brownwell Corporation, and he was a good man. So that's why I said the colored people had a hard time. I was a good man, a good contractor, do good work, and this one white man would take advantage of me, 'cause he was prejudice of me bein' a black man; all the rest of 'em were white contractors.

But don't you know, I had the trouble double, 'cause I was a black man, but lotta times I was mistaken for bein' white—my straight hair and light complexion. A lotta people was always thinkin' that I was white, sometimes. The first real experience I had in the city of Detroit dealin' with racism was when I first come here in the 1920's. The Eastern Market on Russell Street is where truck farmers drive in every mornin' 'fore daybreak and set up stands to sell farm products and produce to dealers and to the public. I was over to the Eastern Market one mornin', and a tall white lady come up to me and said she was hungry and wanted somethin' to eat. She asked did I know where she could get somethin' to eat for twenty-five cents. So I told her I didn't know of any place 'round here in the market where she could get anything to eat for twenty-five cents, but I was fixin' to run my hand in my pocket and give her a quarter, so she could get somethin' for fifty cents. In the meanwhile, I was talkin' while I was reachin' for the quarter, and I said, "You might like to go over on Hastings Street, and I know you will find someplace to eat. I am most sure you can get somethin' over there. I will take you over there if you would like to, missus." (Hastings was two or three blocks away.) She said, "Don't tell me 'bout Hastings . . . Hastings! That's what's the matter with this town now! There's too many damn niggers here!" And she jerked and walked off.

She got away with me so bad! Now I was a Negro, and I was fixin' to give her a quarter; I felt sorry for her. But when she said that, it upset me so much . . . when she walked off, I just looked at her. I felt like runnin' and kickin' her. But I said to myself that wouldn't do any good. She really didn't know I was colored. I said, "Now well, that's the way it is." I thought it's too bad she feels like that.

At another time, I run into a fella and he was from Georgia. He use to work at the express office down in Tennille, Georgia. I met him on the street in Detroit one Sunday, and he said, "That Little Berry?" (They call me Little Berry in Georgia.) The other fella with me, he said, "Yeah." I said, "Yeah, I'm Little Berry." He said, "Well, how do you do? I'm Cox from Georgia." I said, "You're Cox; you're the man that worked at the express office?" He told me he was. I said, "Oh, Mr. Cox, how do you do?" I shook his hand. He was glad to see me, and I was glad to see him. So we talked for a few minutes and I asked him where'bouts was he livin'. He said, "I live in a house up on Eastern Place just 'bout three doors going east off Roosevelt." I said, "Oh, well then, I'll come 'round and stop by to see you sometime." He said, "Well, do that, do that. I would like for you to stop by and see me." He went on, and so I didn't tell him where I lived.

'Bout a week or two later, I had a job workin' over there on Eastern Place, a few doors from where he was livin'. So I thought I would go there and see Mr. Cox. I went on the porch and rang the doorbell and this white lady come to the door; Mr. Cox was a white man. She might have been 'bout seventy or close to it. She couldn't see too well, but when she opened the door and spoke, I said, "Good morning." She said, "Good morning." I said, "Is Mr. Cox here?" She said, "No, he's gone back home." I said, "Where you mean?" She said, "He's gone back to Georgia." I said, "How long he been gone?" She said, "He left a few days ago." I said, "Oh, I'm very sorry; very sorry he's gone. I would have come by and seen him. It's been a couple of weeks ago that I saw him. I was suppose to come 'round and see him."

She said, "You a friend of his?" I said, "Yes, ma'am." She said, "Oh, well, that's too bad that he's gone. Where do you live?" I told her I lived 'cross Hudson on Roosevelt, on Roosevelt near Kirby. "You live over there with those niggers, don'tcha?" she said. "Yes, ma'am." She said, "Well, why don'tcha move over here? We got some houses, a couple of houses over here on Chope, Chope Place here. Tell me, why don't you move in this neighborhood?" I said, "Well, I'll tell you. I have a business over there." She asked me what kinda business. "I have a grocery store and I have a woodyard and coal yard. I sell wood, coal, and all in the grocery store. I sell most everything that you could mention that you eat. I draw a pretty good business from the neighborhood there." She said, "Well, I don't blame you. I would stay right there and get all you can out of 'em, then later on you can move out." I said, "Oh, yes, that's right." She said, "Get all you can out of 'em."

And I thought to myself, well now, I can see now how the white people do. Now she thinks that I am white. That's why she didn't mind me stayin' on her street. So that's the way she felt 'bout it. So I went on, and that was the last of that.

One day, I happened to be down at a drugstore on Warren and Woodward, and my daughter Loucye was with me. She was usin' the phone, and I was in the store. Loucye has very light complexion like me. There were two white fellas standin' over at the fountain. There was a lotta other white people all over the drugstore and another man sittin' at the counter talkin'. He said, "You know one thing? I was down on Hastings the other day. While I was over there, you know one of those niggers cut my pocket outta my coat." One of the others said, "They did?" And then the other man, who was the owner of the store, said, "Well, I'll tell you, I hate those sonofabitches." He said, "I wish they were

113

all dead!" While he was sayin' ". . . I hate those sonofa-bitches . . ." I opened the phone-booth door where Loucye was talkin' on the phone and I said, "Listen, listen, listen!" She stopped talkin' and leaned her head out the door. The man repeated, "I wish they all were dead!" Loucye dropped the phone and rushed out the door and started to say somethin' to that man. And I whispered to her, "Hush, hush, hush, don't say nothin', don't say nothin', just listen." She was full, she was just 'bout to burst. I said, "Don't say nothin' . . . just wait, just wait. There ain't nothin' we can do but just have a argument, and we don't get nowhere." I said, "Just be quiet. You have a chance to learn a lot." And so we went on, and that was the end of that.

When my mother was livin', I use to go down South every winter and stay awhile with her in Georgia. I would go to the train station and show my ticket to the railroad conductor. He would be tellin' people which direction to go and what car to take. He points some people this way and some people the other way. Now, I noticed some people goin' the same way I was goin', but the conductor pointed me a different direction than he pointed out to the other colored people. So I just thought that maybe I was goin' to a different place in Georgia than where they was goin', therefore they'd be ridin' different cars.

So, when I get in the car where the conductor had sent me, why there are nothin' but white people in there. So, now I got to ride on down with 'em. When it come time to eat, I eat right along with 'em. I just thought that happen to be the car I was suppose to ride in accordin' to where I get off at. So I eat and come back to my seat. The train finally pulled into Macon, Georgia.

Well, after I had spent a certain amount of time visitin' my mother and other relatives in the South and started back home to Detroit, we would meet up in Macon at the station. There were colored people there with suitcases and everything, waitin' to come North. I talked with 'em, some were comin' to Detroit and some to Washington and some to Chicago, and places like that. I knew the ones that was comin' to Detroit, and I know we would be ridin' in the same car. So we go out to the conductor and show our tickets. The conductor pointed the other colored people up ahead there in one direction, and he pointed me in the direction back the other way. I went in there and I didn't see nothin' in that car but white people! And so I say to myself, they just didn't know that I was colored. I was sittin' there with those white people all the way. I had to ride all the way; all that evenin', all that night. I knew they didn't know I was a Negro, and I felt miserable! They was makin' a mistake, and I just was miserable!

It was two big white fellas sittin' opposite of me. They was whisperin' to each other and lookin' over at me whisperin'. I felt they knew 'bout who I was. I knew they was talkin' 'bout me. I was reading, and I was lookin' out the corner of my eye. I could see 'em, but they didn't know I was lookin' at 'em. They were talkin' and talkin' and lookin' 'cross the aisle at me, whisperin' to each other. I went on reading my paper. Later on that night, I dozed off and slept a little. I didn't have anybody to talk to, so I just sat there. I thought if I tried to talk to some of 'em, they would find out I was colored. To hear me talk, they would know I was colored. I didn't say nothin' to nobody; I just sat there ridin' along. That mornin', I see the sun begin to raise. I looked out my window; it was daybreak. I got up and stretched, and I walked out and washed my face, then I started walkin'. I walked two or three coaches 'til I found some colored people. When I found the colored people, I went all the way back to where I was sittin', got my suitcase and brought it up there and got seated with the colored people. I just wasn't satisfied sittin' with the whites. I wanted to be with *my* people. When I got up to the colored folks' car, I met somebody goin' to Detroit and different places. We talked and we had a good time, then.

Another time, I was going down to Georgia on the train, and my son George went with me. I had been travelin' on the train and eating. I went in there in the dining room. I didn't sit over behind no curtain and eat; I always sit out in the open, anywhere. I thought the colored people ate anywhere. *I* always go anywhere and eat. I thought all the colored could do it, I didn't know. So, George and I got ready to eat, and we went in the dining room. He is a little shade darker than I am, and we went in there and we sit down to eat.

When we were sittin' there, some fella come there and whispered somethin' to George. George got up and walked out. I thought George had beckoned for the man and asked him where was the restroom or somethin' 'nother, and so I thought he got up and went to the rest room. George stayed out so long, I was sittin' there waitin'. I ordered my food and everything, and George had never come to order his. So, I was fixin' to get ready to eat. I looked 'round and saw George standin' out in the hall in a line with some other colored people. They were standin' behind a curtain, a little curtain hangin' up a couple feet with a room in back of it where the colored people was eatin'. George went over to sit down, but he didn't have no seat; they were crowded out. He was standin' out there, and I got up and went out there and said, "What's the matter? Why didn't you come in and eat?" He said, "The man told me I couldn't eat. They didn't serve colored in there, and I had to eat behind the curtain there." I got mad! I went by the colored people; I had to pass 'em 'fore I got to the white. I said, "If he can't eat, I ain't gonna eat!" The colored folks, they said, "Hush, hush, hush. Don't say nothin', don't say nothin'. " They knowed what it was all 'bout, but I didn't know. They said, "No, no, no, don't say nothin' to those white folks, don't say nothin' to 'em." I was hot!! I was gonna talk to those white folks and let 'em know that George was my son, and if he can't eat, I ain't gonna eat! But the colored folks said, "Naw, naw. Don't say nothin'. Don't say nothin'. Make a fool out of 'em, make a *fool* out of 'em!" So I quieted down, and I went on back to my seat and ate there. And so when George got a seat on the other side where the other colored were, he ate there. The whites never did know who I was. George said that they asked him 'bout was he with me. George said he told 'em naw and acted like he didn't know me. After he found out what it was, he wouldn't expose me. He said naw. Anyway, that's the way they did there, and that shows you how it's just awful . . . awful!!

One time when I went down South, I drove! My daughter Loucye and one of her girl friends went with us. We had left home early that mornin' little 'fore day, maybe 'bout four or five o'clock in the mornin'. So we got somewhere in Ohio and Loucye and her friend say, "Where are we going to eat, Papa?" I said, "We gonna eat just anywhere we find a place open, anywhere we find a place open. Let me know when you see a place where we can stop." Then Loucye said, "There is a place to eat, but I don't think we can eat in there. I don't think they'll serve colored in there." I said, "Aw, sho', they'll serve colored anywhere *I* go. They serve colored anywhere." Loucye said, "I don't know. I don't know 'bout us going in there." I said, "Aw, come on, come on."

I explained to 'em why they don't serve colored most of the time. It's 'cause some of 'em go into a eatin' place, and the first thing they say is "Do you serve colored?" The colored give 'em the chance to say they don't serve colored. "All you got to do is go in there and sit down and order what you want, just like you was white. Just order what you want, and they will serve you," I said. But that's the trouble with our people, they gonna *ask* 'em do they serve colored. All you got to do is go in there and order what you want, sit there, and they'll bring it to you. Sure 'nuff, we did and they did.

The next day we got to Georgia in a suburb of Atlanta, Georgia. They said, "Papa, we want to eat, we're kinda hungry. You said we can eat anyplace, so the next eating place you get to, let's stop." I said, "Sure, we can eat anywhere." We got to a restaurant and Loucye says, "There's a place, Papa." I pulled out and stopped there. Since we was anxious to get on down to Sandersville, we decided I would get the food and bring it out. I seen the white people goin' in the door, and I went on in the door with 'em. I went on in and ordered three hamburgers and three cups of coffee. I could look through into the kitchen, and I saw a colored lady in there beckonin' for me to come in there. I thought maybe she was some old friend of ours that knew me years back and wanted to talk with me. I thought maybe she knew me. So, as soon as I paid the waitress for the hamburgers, I went between the counter and went on out in the back in the kitchen.

I was lookin' for the cook to say, "Is that you, Berry?" or somethin' like that. But instead, she didn't say a word to me. She was just lookin' down and kept on cookin'. I thought when she get through, she was gonna talk with me. When she got through, she wrapped the hamburgers up and give 'em to me. I started back through to the front of the store. She said, "Uh-uh, you can't go that way." I said, "Can't go what way . . . why?" She said, "Naw, naw, they don't allow you to go that way. You got to go out the back." I said, "Out the back! Now I come in that way." She said, "Yeah, but you can't go back through there." That was the *colored* lady talkin'! I started to go anyhow; but I said to myself, "Maybe she know somethin', and since I didn't know, maybe I'll just take her word." So I wouldn't start nothin', even though I sure wanted to go back out the front. But, I thought, maybe I'll just go on out the back door.

I got out back there, and there was a high, tall wire fence out there; I looked for the gate. I said, "How's I'm gonna get out? Where's the gate?" She said, "Haven't got no gate." I said, "How am I gonna get out?" She said, "Get over the fence." I said, "I can't take this food over that fence!" She said, "I'll hand it to you." So I went and climbed up and got over the fence and reached up to the top, and she handed the food to me over the fence. Now I looked 'round in the alley, and it was closed up on each side by a plank fence all the way down the alley. Looked like it was 'bout two blocks long 'fore you could get outta that alley; nailed up. Now I got to walk way to the end of the alley to get out.

Loucye and her girl friend kept a-watchin' for me to come out the front door. It was so long 'fore I come out, they was wonderin' what become of me. I had to go way up the alley and come 'cross the street over there and come down to the other side. Then after a while, I walked up on the opposite side of 'em. They were lookin' for me on one side of the car, the way I left there, and I walked up to 'em on the other. They said, "Papa! Where you come from? We thought you went in there." I said, "I did go in there." They said, "Well, where you coming from this-a-way?" I said, "Well, they didn't want me to come back out the front door." They went to laughin', laughin'. I said, "Well, I'll tell you, the colored lady, she is the one told me. I think I could have come out the front door, but it was the colored lady who told me don't go out the front door. She was tryin' to help me." Then, I told 'em 'bout the high fence I had to climb. Oh, they just laughed and laughed. The white people didn't say nothin' to me. The colored lady, she knew I was colored, but maybe the white didn't know it. But colored people know colored people, anyhow. You might fool some of the white, but the colored know when you are colored. Anyway, we had a lotta fun from that one time, there.

CHAPTER ELEVEN

Wher I first come to Detroit, I didn't know anything 'bout politics and political business. There was a good friend of mine who was one of the leadin' members of my church, and he was a captain for some political candidate. I had a good business goin' and had a lotta people workin' for me. So, when people would come to Detroit from Georgia, Mississippi, Alabama, or Tennessee, or somewhere from the southern states, the people at the church would send 'em to me for me to give 'em jobs as mechanics. They made good mechanics. There was lots of 'em that I give jobs to.

Brother Jones knew I had a lotta influence with the people, and he wanted me to help him in his campaign work. This was the first time I ever did campaign work. He took me all 'round to different places: upstairs, downstairs, downtown, different places. He had me to meet his candidate and seven or eight other candidates. I didn't know anything 'bout what was goin' on. I asked him if these were good men. He said, "Oh, yes, good men, good men!" I took his word. I just believed whatever he said, and I worked for his candidates.

He and I went around and left literature here and there. We went to every place on our list. We went 'round to the different booths where they was votin'. So, after we had done all this, Brother Jones said to me, "Now, when the election is over, you go back around to all these candidates where we went today and you'll get some money." I said, "Money for what?" He said, "For workin' with me for them." I said, "I wasn't chargin' 'em any money. I thought you said they was good men." He said, "They are good men." I said, "Well, they gonna pay you for workin'?" He told me yeah. I said, "I thought they was good men, and we was gonna put 'em in office on account of they are good men to do a good job in the office." He said, "Aw, don't worry 'bout that. Get the money, get the money." I said, "Well, let me tell you one thing. If we go 'round and work for these people and they aren't any good for our race of people and they pay us some money for workin' for 'em, they don't owe us anything else."

I said, "Now, suppose they have so many hundreds or thousands of jobs to give out, and we have people here that is capable of doin' those jobs. We have children that come out of school, scholars that you know is capable for some of the jobs. And you go down there to get 'em placed in those jobs, and the people that paid you off act like they don't know you and won't pay you any attention . . . I wouldn't do nothin' like that; that is just out of reason." I said, "If you work and get a candidate elected just to collect *money*, and the candidate is no good, now, we got to be contented with those people even if they're rotten people 'til their time in office is out. We don't get no consideration; they don't have to do anything for our people. Naw, I don't do that kinda business!" After then, I cut loose from him. I didn't work with him anymore. I didn't go back anywhere to see 'bout gettin' any money from any of those candidates.

But after that, I continued to be interested whenever people run for office. I always liked to work in politics. I always wanted to get good men in whatever offices was open for election, 'cause I knew if you get good people in office, then you don't have to worry 'bout gettin' justice. 'Cause they will give everybody a fair deal if they're good people. Don't help put nobody in office just to do you a favor. I feel that if the people who get in office give you justice, then they give you a chance to make your livin'. You're not lookin' for somebody to come and just give you somethin'. I never did look for that.

Whether it's a job or political office, we have a lotta qualified people that go down to qualify. But on account of things like the color of your skin, you can't get the job. I always read up on candidates to find out what I could do 'bout 'em. I watch 'em and talk with 'em. If

I feel like they're good people, I go out and work for 'em without any charges. I didn't charge 'em anything! I never charged nobody anything that I've ever worked for. The first colored one I worked for was the old man Senior Diggs, who was runnin' for state senator the first time. I had been doin' some work on his property, the Diggs Funeral Home. And he asked me to work for him on his campaign. I'd go 'round—like when the election day came—I would take my car and go down and pick up people and take 'em to the booth to vote. I'd pick up these people and I'd talk, I'd ask 'em to vote for Mr. Diggs.

'Bout the end of 1929 the Depression came and I had to quit the Brownwell Corporation, on account they didn't have enough work and then went bankrupt. I always continued to work some all through the Depression. I had to work. I had a little job here and a little job there. I got on with the city as a carpenter, I think, for three days. I was gettin' 'bout eighteen dollars for those three days. Then along the side, I'd pick up some little money from jobs people give me. They'd have a little patch job here and a little patch job there.

But what it really come down to, I was hustlin' hard. I knew I had to feed my wife and children, my family. I was scufflin', scufflin' hard. We was always able to get shoes for the children, but it was tough. Everything was tough. I never did look to get on the Welfare, and I had a right 'cause I was a taxpayer and everything. I just kept a-shiftin' 'round, makin' a little money here, a little money there, and I just kept on like that long as I could. Then, it got so that all my help was gone. The jobs I was gettin' wasn't big enough for me to pay my men, and I didn't have nothin' for 'em to do. So they all went on the Welfare to get money to help 'em out, feed their families.

My wife, Bertha, she had little jobs, too. She went off to do a little work. And we'd have to get somebody to stay with the children. Fact, all through the Depression, we had somebody to help take care of the children. At the first beginnin', Bertha worked at an office. I don't know what kinda work she was doin', but she was doin' daywork of some kind. But so with the both of us workin', it still wasn't enough. Times was just hard! Now I was doin' everything I could to make a livin'. I was sellin' ice, coal, wood—even collectin' junk paper to sell. I bought watermelons and sold 'em whole and by the slice. Ol' Man Mr. Keith, who lived down the street from us on Hudson Street, told me two or three times that I was workin' too hard and even though I was a young man I could break myself down. They say his baby boy, Damon, is now a judge in the high court.

But I was shiftin'. I'd always do things. So we kept on like that long as we could, but then I had to go down to see the welfare people. But I held out; stood it long as I could. And everybody was down there. Then, when I did finally go down there to the Welfare, some of the people saw me. They told me that I didn't need any help. Said, "That man use to work; he's got a business; he's a big man." Well, there was a time I was kinda big. I had people workin' for me and all. But 'cause of the Depression and bein' that there wasn't no more work, all that went down. I wasn't no big man; I was like the rest of 'em. I knew I had a right to be on welfare, in my condition, as much as the rest of 'em. But the people down there at the welfare office said I couldn't get on. My business was the reason keepin' me off of the Welfare.

So I had to go down to city hall. I had to talk with the secretary of the mayor. The lady told me, "Well, go back and bring in all your business papers: receipts, bankbook, and everything." So I did. I had to carry all of that stuff down there. I laid 'em out 'fore her, and she saw, was checkin' what I been doin' for years back . . . my bankbook where I had punched holes through it when I got all my money out, just everything. When she got through lookin' through my papers, she said, "Well, Mr. Gordy, I'm going to give you a note to take back to the welfare office." She said, "I see here the history of what your business used to be and what it is now. I'll give you this letter to take back. If there was just twelve men of your race like you, who would stand up like you do, your people would have it better, get somewhere." I said, "Yes, ma'am." That's all I said. And so she give me the letter, and I went back down there.

See, she was helpin' me out, sure 'nuff. I went back to the Welfare, and I didn't have no more trouble, then.

So I got on. I had all my eight children and all to feed. And so I didn't have no trouble with 'em. I didn't know what the lady wrote in the letter, but they treated me all right after then. Some of the people in line there, they didn't think I should be on there, and they tried to block me from gettin' on there. But after the lady found out 'bout my business, how I took care of business, and now how things was, well, she was glad to send the letter over there to take care of me. The people at the office there was very polite when I went back. But they was tough on me before. But one thing, I told 'em that soon I'd get to where I could get off, 'cause I really didn't want to be on welfare!

So what happened right 'bout that time during the Depression, my father-in-law, he sent us a hundred dollars up here. He said that's what he got for two of my cows from my home down there in Georgia. And we was so happy! I wish he'd sold all of 'em! We got that hundred dollars; seemed like *five hundred* dollars at that time. That hundred dollars was big money in the Depression years. But then again, I thought anything was good money! So he sent us a hundred dollars, and that's what I got out of those cows. We had left everything there in Georgia, everything. Everybody come—first come, first serve—and took the pork, cows, and I didn't get hardly anything for it. So then I decided I'd rent out the houses down there on the plantation; I'd heard some people was there and ruinin' the houses.

I started to rent those two houses on the plantation for six dollars a month. I rented out houses down there for six dollars a month, and I was payin' fifty dollars up here for my house! I thought that was out of reason! But I made out with it. I made it by scufflin' hard, and so that's one way we made it 'til we got in better shape.

CHAPTER TWELVE

My father-in-law, Mr. Burton F. Fuller, still lived in Milledgeville, Georgia. He had a lotta people farming for him. Well, Mr. Fuller got sick, and my wife and her sister and brothers arranged for him to be brought to Detroit. It seemed like he wasn't gonna get well, so he decided to have me go down South and sell out everything he had down there, except his land and property. He wanted me to sell his cotton and what other crops he had made that year. He had sharecroppers on his plantation that owed him money, too.

I told my father-in-law, if he would give me the power of attorney, where I would have authority to do certain things, I would go back down South and close his farm out for him. Sure 'nuff, he gave me a list of everybody he owed money to, including the bank. He also had some cows on his farm that belonged to me. During a dry year in Georgia, I had him to move my cows up to his plantation in Milledgeville. He had good pasture on his plantation, so he kept my cows and raised 'em for me.

When I got down there to see 'bout his estate, the first thing I did was to sell all my cows which I had left with him. Then I set out to sell his cotton. I had the cotton hauled into town. The man I was sellin' the cotton to weighed it up and gave me a slip to go and pick up the money for the cotton. When I got to the cashier, he didn't want to pay me! He said some other fellas who lived on Mr. Fuller's plantation had owed another white man some money. They wanted me to pay off the debts of those other fellas, too, bein' that they lived on my father-in-law's plantation. I told him I had no authority to do that. The cashier said, "Well, you can't get the money for this cotton." I said, "Well, you have a right to give me a check. I sold the cotton, and they gave me a slip for you to write the check out." But he said those other fellas owed this certain white man so much money. He said, "And I will not pay you unless you pay off that debt." I told him I didn't have no authority to do that, and I ain't got nothin' to do with what this tenant owed anybody. I said, "I only have orders to carry out my father-in-law's wishes." And so he still wouldn't pay me for the cotton.

I went to a judge, who was a good friend of my father-in-law, and I told him what the man was doin'. I told the judge I didn't have no right to pay nobody else's debts, 'cause Mr. Fuller didn't tell me to. Mr. Fuller told me what debts to pay, and I'm gonna pay those debts and that's all. I told the judge that the man's got my cotton tied up there, and he won't pay me. I said, "It's been sold, but the man who writes the checks won't write my check out." The judge said, "Well, I can't do anything 'bout it myself, but I'll send you over to see this lawyer." He gave me the lawyer's name, and everything. Mr. Watson. The judge called Mr. Watson, the lawyer, up and told him I would be over there. And so I went over to see the lawyer in Milledgeville.

I explained the whole thing to the lawyer. He picked up the phone and called up this fella that was holdin' my check and asked him 'bout it. The check writer said he was to hold the cotton and the check 'til this other white man got his money. I heard the lawyer say, "Well, you can't do that." Then the lawyer asked me, "How much more cotton you got to gather up yet?" I told him, "Well, I don't think very much more, just a little remnants and a little scatterin' of a bale." Then the lawyer told him somethin' that I didn't tell him. He said to the man, "Well, he got another bale coming. You can get your money outta that." The lawyer just wanted the check writer to turn my check loose. The cashier agreed to pay me for the cotton he was holdin'. So I went on back there and as soon as I walked up, the cashier handed me the check.

I always thank people for everything they do for me. But after he give me this check, I was kinda mad, since he had made so much trouble for me. I just took the check and didn't say thanks at all. I just took the check and just walked on out. I thought 'bout it as I was walkin' . . . that with my back turned, he's liable to shoot me in the back. I kinda turned my head crossways and looked out the corner of my eye. I could see he had stood up and was just lookin' at me real straight. I walked on and got outta the front door. I got in the car as quick as I could and left there! Then I went on and I sold out everything Mr. Fuller had there as quickly as I could and got away from town. They couldn't stop me at all.

When I went back down South 'bout a year later, I saw the Reverend there. He asked me had anybody told me anything 'bout the high sheriff there in town. I told him, "No, nobody told me anything 'bout no sheriff." He said, "Well, they was talkin' 'bout it down at the church. They told somebody to tell you not to come back down here anymore." I said, "Why?" He said, "Well, now the white people said that you was tryin' to be smart down here. And if you were to come back down here, they was goin' to see 'bout you." He went on to tell me that the high sheriff had killed two or three colored people 'round there, business people. He wanted me to kinda get away from down there. I went down to my sister's, and I told her what this man had told me. I said, "Well, I don't know 'bout it. But the Reverend said Brother Johnny Williams knowed 'bout it, and he was suppose to tell me." I said, "Well, I went by Brother Williams' place the other day when

I first got here. I was in his field where he was pickin' cotton, and he didn't say anything 'bout it." And so I decided to go up there and ask him 'bout it.

I drove back up to Brother Williams', 'bout fifteen miles away. When I asked him 'bout it, he said he witnessed it. He said, "Oh, yes, Mr. So-and-so said that you, Berry, were tryin' to be smart. You come down here tryin' to be smart, and if you come back down here again, what he was goin' to do to you." I said, "Well, you know I was out in the field the other day talkin' with you, Brother Williams, and the sheriff told you 'bout it." I said, "I could have got killed! Why *you* didn't tell me 'bout it?" He said, "Well, you know how it is. I don't believe in havin' nothin' to do with other people's affairs." I said, "Well, Brother Williams, I'll tell you. If a man had said that 'bout you, I would have been 'blige to tell you 'bout it." He said, "Well, Brother Gordy, you know how these people are and how it is down here? I just didn't want to be into nothin'." I said, "Well, okay then." So I left him standin' there.

That's the way those colored people are down there. They are so scared of those white folks 'til, if they say they are gonna do somethin' to you, they're feared to tell you 'bout it. And so I went on back and told my sister it's true.

Well, my sister got scared; she didn't want me to go back through Milledgeville. She wanted me to go a different route and leave there right away. But I had to go back through there to pick up a girl I was suppose to bring back to Detroit. I had promised a friend of mine to carry the girl back to work in his store. This was a man I had known all my life. I knew his father and mother, and we all went to school together. I had made the arrangements, and she was all ready to come back with me. So I had to go back through Milledgeville. My sister didn't want me to do it. I told her I could go through there, pick the girl up, and go 'head on at night. And sure 'nuff, I did. 'Bout eleven o'clock one night, I went through town, picked the girl up, and pulled out to Detroit. I made it. I made it all right.

I'll tell you, I remember the first time I went on an airplane. I said I never would ride a airplane. I just didn't think . . . get up that high, you didn't know what's gonna happen! I said I wouldn't fly in no airplane. I always felt like that. I'd just travel in cars, bus, or train; never did think I'd ride a airplane.

But I got a telephone call, tellin' me that my sister Lula was sick. They wanted me to come down at once to Georgia. I'd been drivin' in my car all the time, and I told 'em, well, it would take me a couple of days. But my sister was sick and had some business she wanted me to take care of; she wanted me to come down earlier. I asked 'em would it be all right if I leave and be there a couple of days from now, and they said no. "You'd better come now, while she can talk," they said. So I knew she must be very sick. I thought I'd better rush quick as I could. I said, well, in a case like this, I think I'm gonna take a chance on the airplane. I just made up my mind to ride the plane.

So I got my ticket and I got on the plane. At that time, I didn't see no colored on there but me. And so the plane was suppose to leave at a certain time, and it didn't leave then. The man come in, the announcer, and told us to hold on, the wait will be 'bout ten minutes. They kept us sittin' there. After while, he come back and said, "Well, there's a little more trouble than they thought. Now it's gonna be twenty minutes 'fore we can get goin'." Then I got to studyin' while sittin' on that plane. I was studyin' whether I should go on that plane. And I got my suitcase, and I walked to the door. I started to get off, not go on that plane! And everybody else was sittin' so quiet. So, I thought, if I get off the plane, then after while they gonna get goin'. They might be talkin' 'bout "That nigger got off!" I was Negro and I'm the only one that left. So, I was standin' by the door by myself, kinda frightened 'bout things. Maybe if somethin' did happen, they'd say, "That Negro was the only one smart enough to get off." But I studied it, and I wouldn't get off then. I decided to stick it out.

Sure 'nuff, later on they got goin'. They told me if there's gonna be any danger on the plane, there's a red light that come on. So, I sit there just watchin' that red light all the time! I didn't sleep any, just watchin' that red light that means danger. One time I got a little drowsy, looked, and thought I saw that red light come on! I jumped up and looked again. It was nothin'. So then I made it, made it to Atlanta.

When I got there, then I had to take another little small plane to Macon, Georgia. I got on the plane, and

I could hear it skippin'; it was skippin'—*putt, putt, putt, putt*—like it oughta stop! I was uneasy 'bout that. So, I got to Macon and my nephew was there. He told me that the plane had a skip in it, and I said, "Sure, I heard that skip in it, and I was worried 'bout it!" I was sure glad to be down on the ground. Since that time, I got use to 'em. I get on a plane, and I don't worry now. But I'm always very happy to get back on land again. Now that's the way it is 'bout the planes.

CHAPTER THIRTEEN

When I was young, we would get up early every mornin' and go to work. We were real healthy. And it's good to be healthy. And I say now, after people grow up with good health, they oughta have sense enough to know how to take care of 'emselves after they get grown.

I listened to the old people, and so I learned that whenever they tell me somethin' 'bout what is wrong or right, I just believed 'em. My mother and 'em, they taught us a lotta things, and I believed whatever they said.

Fresh air is one of the greatest things you can have as a medicine. Fresh air is always good anytime. It's not good to close up where you can't get any fresh air. And that is one reason I think people in the southern states, especially out in the country, is so healthy. I'm sure that's some of the cause of it. They're very healthy. I know on the farm they always get plenty of fresh air all the time, 'cause the houses is not so tight. They always can see the sunrise without gettin' outta their beds— through the cracks in the house.

One thing 'bout a lotta people, they're afraid of the cold weather. When they go outside, and they know it's cold, they tighten their skin up 'fore they go out. They walk out and when the air strike 'em, they draw up and tighten their skin and their blood can't circulate through their body so well. They're scared of cold; they're just scared of it! If you just relax, just relax, and let your blood circulate, you won't get near as cold. I learned that whenever you think it's cold outside and you tighten up your skin, your blood doesn't circulate well, and you gonna be chilly. But if you go outside and relax and with your blood circulating good, you don't get near as cold. So the way I go along now, I don't take as heavy a coat and I feel good.

I found that if you bathe in warm water all the time, your body is already warm, and when you first strike the cold air, it'll chill you through, and you gotta put on aplenty of clothes. The cold-water baths really make a difference. I'll admit, it's pretty hard bathin' in the *cold water*, but I think you find out if you did, people would have less sickness. It is hard to do. Course, I had experienced it. When I was in the army, I learned it is good to stand more cold. But it was hard for me to get back to takin' those cold showers. And I imagine it's gonna be hard for you, if you never did it before. Any-

139

thing anybody haven't had the experience in doin', it's a little hard to do. But I think cold-water bathin' will help you rid off a lotta sickness.

Another thing to keep you healthy is don't smoke. I don't smoke cigarettes. Oh, one time I did try some rabbit tobacco. That's some stuff you grow. I went out back of our house and wrapped some up, a little bit, in some paper. I lit it to see if I could smoke it. I took 'bout two draws of it, and my head got dizzy. I threw it away! And that's all the smokin' I ever did! I never did like it.

When I was young, a little boy, I saw a man demonstrate what smokin' cigarettes does to you. He said that smokes are no good for your lungs, and he demonstrated it. He took a white handkerchief and took a draw off a cigarette, then he blew his breath on this handkerchief. You could see a yella stain on it. He said, "You see this stain here? Every time you inhale the smoke there, this stain gets on your lungs; time after time, day and night. It just continues on." He tell me that so much of this stuff gathers, it forms sort of a crusty thickness like on your lungs. So, anytime I found out somethin' and believed somethin' is against me, I leave it go.

I've seen fellas drink, and that's another thing I fight against. I come to know that drinkin' whiskey is not good. I've seen four people killed 'cause of drinkin'. I tell people 'bout drinkin', too. You hear some of 'em say, "Well, I don't drink much. I don't drink much." I try to stop 'em. They say, "I don't drink. I just drink a little bit to be sociable." I say, "Well, that's just it.

140

That's where a lotta it start. You drink a little bit to be sociable."

Now, being sociable, it's okay to drink a little; if you know when to quit! But as you drink a little bit to be sociable, and it kinda gets into your head, you get to staggerin', feelin' a little wobbly. You feel good and lively, and it takes all your shame and fear away. Whiskey has you thinkin' that you're worth everything, but you're really not worth anything!! It has you thinkin' you can turn the world upside down. But you can't do anything! It's just somethin' to fool you and make you think you are what you're not. The whiskey just layin' there to fool you!

Now, about growin' up and learnin' as you grow. You think when you 'bout fifteen, you just know it all. You think, "Oh, no, I know everything, can't nobody fool me!" Now, when you get to be twenty you find out you didn't know so much when you were fifteen. Now, you think, "I can outsmart anybody I know." You think you be outsmartin' older people, but the people who have went along ahead of you, they been all along the way. They know just 'bout what you are thinkin'. They know at each stage just 'bout how a person feels, 'cause they have had that experience. Traveling this life is somethin' like traveling on a highway. You know 'bout the part of life's highway that you have traveled on, and you can look back there and you can tell some younger people what's gonna happen. But if you haven't traveled the road yourself, you can't tell what's gonna happen.

Now, as I always said, "You can give without loving, but you cannot love without giving." You'll find this to be true. Now, if you love a person, that person don't have to ask you for favors. They don't have to ask you for this or that or whatever you have. You just want to give it to 'em, anyway. You just love 'em. You just want to always try to do somethin' for 'em.

So, another thing 'bout worryin', I stopped thinkin' 'bout how old I am long time ago. One time my son and I went to play golf at the golf course. It cost a dollar and a half for admission. When we went to pay, the lady asked me how old I was. She explained to me that if I was a certain age, I could shoot for fifty cents; save a dollar. I was glad to give her my age, I didn't care how old I was. She then asked for my driver's license to check it and found out that I was two years older than the age I give her. My son fell out laughin', and it tickled me, too. I tried to put it up to the top, so I could save the dollar, and come to find out that I told her two years younger than I was.

Anyway, I feel young and I feel healthy. And I always take care of myself. I met some little boys the other day, and so I was talkin' with 'em. I always liked to talk with little children, boys, that be 'round. These little kids, they stopped and talked to me out in front of my house. There was four of 'em. One of 'em said, "Mister, how old are you?" I said, "Well, how old do you think I am?" He looked at me and said, "Thirty-five!" I said, "Well, you're a good guesser; you're a very good guesser." And the other one, he said, "No, he ain't thirty-five; he's forty-five!" I said, "Well, you guess pretty good, too. Ya'all guessed pretty well." And then the third one said, "No, he'd older than that, he's about sixty years old." That's the largest boy's guess. I said, "Well, you're not so bad yourself!"

There's another little boy standin' there. Seemed like he was 'bout four years or smaller. I didn't think he could count more than 'bout twenty or thirty or somethin' like that. I just said, "Well now, here's a boy . . ." I was gonna have fun outta him, for him to guess my age. I knew he was gonna put it way down 'cause he couldn't count too much. He was too young to know much 'bout forty, fifty, or sixty; twenty or thirty, he might know 'bout that. I said, "Well here now, here's a boy; he knows my age." I said, "Whatever this boy says, that's how old I am. Okay, well now, sonny, how old am I?" He looked at my feet, and he looked at my head, and then he looked back down, and then he said, "You is a hundred years old!" Then all of 'em looked amazed, and they said, "Mister, you a hundred years old!?" I said, "You heard what the boy said, didn't you?" And they said, "Ooh, a hundred, a hundred!" They all ran off, then down the street yellin', "A hundred, a hundred, a hundred years old!!" That's what they yelled; they was so surprised!

And so if anybody hears that I'm a hundred years

old . . . I know the rumor's gone out that I'm a hundred years old, 'cause they gonna tell it to everybody. So, if I ever hear it again, I know exactly where it come from. The little boy said I was a hundred years old; that was the understanding he had. And so that's what I'm goin' for . . . one hundred years old.

Berry Gordy, Sr., died November 21, 1978.
He was ninety years old.